Talk Is Cheap
The Digital PR Your Startup Needs
(*But Can't Afford*)

LEANNE ROSS

Copyright © 2016 Leanne Ross

All rights reserved.

ISBN: 1530402360
ISBN-13: 978-1530402366

Cover Illustration: Oran Kane

ABOUT THE AUTHOR

Leanne Ross is a Digital Communicator, Accredited Member of the Chartered Institute of Public Relations, Member of the Chartered Institute of Marketing and Commended in the CIPR 2015 Outstanding Young Communicator Award in Ireland.

Supporting small businesses and startups to improve their overall Communications and, ultimately, their bottom line, Leanne has also assisted many PR Agencies to do likewise for their clients as the industry moves evermore into the digital sphere.

She writes a blog (www.aCupOfLee.com) on the Irish Communications industry, guest lectures at the University of Ulster and is a regular guest speaker, industry trainer and mentor to young entrepreneurs.

She lives in Belfast with her New Zealand-born husband and her son.

You can follow Leanne on Twitter @aCupOfLee

CONTENTS

    Warning

    Foreword

1	PR Media Relations	1
2	Imagery	26
3	Events	35
4	Awards	42
5	Desk Drops	49
6	Digital Communications	54
7	Social Media Marketing	61
8	Blogging for Business	88
9	Blogger Outreach	105
10	Email Marketing	114
11	Social Media Networking	121
12	Evaluation	129
13	Outsourcing	140

WARNING

Welcome to my book. Before I get started imparting a decade's worth of PR industry advice, there are a few things I think you should know:

1. Everything You Will Read Here Exists Online

I don't want you to feel cheated. If you searched long and hard enough online you would find it all. To be honest, that's how most of the industry learned what we know. But the internet is a big place. And it's full of Charlatans. The point of arming yourself with this book is to be efficient with your resources - both time and money. I have combined everything I know, and everything the people I learn from know, into one place.

2. Not Everything You Will Read Here Exists Online

I'm contradicting myself already, apologies. What I mean by this is that all of the theory I'm combining has been discussed in multiple ways on many channels before. However, *the practical guide* to actually implementing these strategies yourself is not usually handed over to anyone outside the intern desk of a PR Agency.

3. I Have Not Lost My Mind

That's what you're thinking. If everyone else in the industry is holding back the last piece of the puzzle or charging three and four figure retainers to deliver it, why would I be giving it away in a book?

Because I believe the Communications industry is transforming. Not everyone in it is secure enough in their abilities to lay all their cards on the table and show the extent of what they know.

Because the boom of startups and entrepreneurs in today's society is bursting with people more than capable of doing their own PR, in my opinion. But I still back myself to deliver the work better than an amateur, should a company find itself with the resources to hire me.

Because I don't believe in keeping Digital PR elusive to the masses like some kind of Dark Art. Or charging through the roof for it.

You can do your own Digital Communications and PR, with enough time and effort, after reading this book. To what level you can do it is the variable you will discover. If you feel you need better, then you are informed enough to source a specialist to deliver it for you.

If after reading this, you know what you need, and what it's *really* worth, before you buy it, then your investment has been returned.

FOREWORD

This book took a mere few months to complete.

Don't close it yet - that's not a reflection of the quality of the content!

So why tell you?

Well partly because you should know that I have only decided to compile a book having already spent years publishing what I know to the world on a PR industry blog. Avid readers asked me to pull all the advice together into one place. So I started to do that.

Then it changed.

I realised that I had the opportunity to give away all that I know. Not just tasters to get clients in the door, like a lot of company blogs do. But the very A-Z of tasks that I would do when I'm working for a client, or doing media relations for a PR agency subcontracting to me, or creating content for a digital agency doing likewise.

But why would I do such a thing?

Because I believe that the Dark Art of PR is dying.

The murky worlds of Digital Marketing and PR are now overlapping in an aggressive attempt to steal each other's pay day. That's where Digital Communications comes in. That's what I do. I merge both disciplines, with a knowledgable foot in each camp, understanding how they work together, for mutual benefit.

You see, Digital Marketers are very good at using their technical skills to bring you a return on investment spend online. That's why their social media results are so impressive; they have the budgets and know-how to grow audiences and bring in sales through things like Facebook ads and Google PPC targeting. It requires technical knowledge of the platforms. That's what you pay Digital Agencies for.

I can't teach you to do that. I'll always tell you to outsource it.

Granted, PR Agencies have a slightly harder task luring website visitors and sales leads organically (for free) through digital and social media content, on top of traditional media relations, an already resource-intensive job.

But they're having to do all that extra digital work to stay current and deliver what the modern business needs in terms of communicating where its audience is: online.

The problem for the PR industry - and the mammoth opportunity for you in the business community - is that the online media landscape is drastically different to the days of old. All the secrets to Do-It-Yourself have now been exposed. Journalists no longer have PR gatekeepers and even when they do, they'd rather talk to you anyway.

And the other big problem is that the majority of the PR industry is a little behind in digital know-how. I know this because I get called in a lot to teach them. They're learning. They're probably reading this book. Just like you. You're not paying for secret information or elusive contacts anymore.

Everything outside of media relations can be learned by following digital industry leaders online, which is also - coincidentally - where all the journalists are. That's how most of us keep our skills and contacts up-to-date.

So nowadays you often pay a PR retainer for time resource and experience more than skill or contacts. Otherwise someone more important than the junior account executives would be ringing journalists to place your story.

An agency or consultant can still sometimes do a better job for you simply because they are more experienced and, therefore, faster. They immediately know media outlets. They are creative by nature, brainstorming ideas by the second. They make less mistakes.

However, in the bootstrapping days for startups, small businesses and entrepreneurs - when you really need media coverage, SEO and a social presence - there is no reason why you can't do a perfectly decent job yourself.

Well, there is *one* reason.

You are time-poor. And the internet is a big place.

Our quest for digital media coverage and search engine brownie points has led us to fill the internet with fluff. Wading through it is time-consuming, even for those of us who must trawl it for trustworthy industry information on a daily basis.

So I'm bringing together the best of what I know, in a succinct, easy-to-follow format. Fluff free.

Your next question, undoubtedly then is, why me?

For a start, I have used the very steps within this book to build my own career. I went from just another "PR girl" to a local industry leading voice by the age of 30. Does that make me the best? Not necessarily. But it makes me the best at promoting myself and that brings me business. Just like you're trying to do.

Through a mix of blogging, media relations, social media networking and industry award entries - all PR tactics included in this book - I built a flourishing freelance career in a crowded market.

So I now find myself working predominantly with startups, small businesses and social enterprises and I know this much to be true:

- You can't afford massive PR retainers
- Even if you could afford a basic retainer, it wouldn't be worth much more than two handfuls of hours a month to the over-worked modern agency. It won't buy you a lot that you couldn't achieve yourself

- Most entrepreneurs have the skill set required to do the work themselves once they find out who to contact (because you're already the best at pitching your business)
- The modern media can be found and pitched more quickly and easily than ever before and digital media is hungry for stories
- Most journalists would much rather hear from a company founder than a PR person any day of the week

This book is aimed at just this type of person - the self-starter, passionate-owner, experienced-pitcher. You.

You will have a basic knowledge of social and digital, which is the cornerstone of modern Digital PR and Inbound Marketing. You will have set up a Facebook page or you will have used Twitter (if not, you will do so soon and there are plenty of free articles online to guide you through the basic steps).

You'll be used to selling your business and you'll be keen to look for opportunities to promote it. This book is structured so that you can read it front-to-back or dip into any relevant section as a standalone, depending on what tactics you want to try.

"But I won't be able do it!" I hear some of you cry.

Let me assure you that your insecurity is lying to you, and most of my industry would be quite happy to feed that insecurity to keep themselves in a job.

Since starting my own business I have realised that the hurdles most business owners overcome makes them ideal PR pros.

You have to seek out information when you don't know where to start. You have to digest and implement technical processes (like financial regulations) which may be outside your comfort zone. Then you have to hire staff and deal with everything from recruitment to pensions. That's on top of your product or service, which is probably the only bit of the business that comes naturally to you.

If you can run a business, you can teach yourself PR.

End of discussion with internal insecurity.

And even if you're just founding a startup from your bedroom or you have been in business decades but want to become a thought leader in your industry - the fact is you sought this information. You found me. You invested in developing yourself by buying the book.

Trust me; in an industry that is largely self-taught and based primarily on the natural ability to communicate, with a big dose of initiative on top, you're already halfway there.

Of course once you're successful enough (i.e. you have enough money), then it makes sense to outsource all of this work on basic economics alone - when your hourly rate is worth more than the PR person you outsource the work to then it's no longer worth your time.

Until then, it's just you. Or your small team.

And I've got your back.

Leanne

1 PR MEDIA RELATIONS

> **"The media landscape is changing. The way to find your place in it remains largely the same. Only now, the gatekeepers aren't as important."**

PR now encompasses a breadth of communication disciplines but it has always, and still does predominantly, involve traditional media relations.

Indeed, it's the aspect of the job for which the industry is most recognised and, subsequently, most derided.

Despite the massive changes to our media landscape, mainstream media coverage (like newspapers, radio and TV) is still one of the most effective ways of achieving PR goals. It remains the cornerstone to gaining credibility, retaining reputation and communicating with your audience.

That's because despite fears over the decline in printed publications and the rise of social media, online paywalls and ad-blockers, news media remains one of the public's most trusted sources of information.

However, competing for column inches or airtime isn't easy, especially if what you're promoting isn't the most exciting or easily-understood thing in the world.

But it is easier than it used to be. Finding journalists is more straight forward, methods of contacting them more simple and, because we're all bombarded with communications messages, they want your pitch to be short and snappy. Just like the pitches you may have given to the bank, potential investors, or the elevator pitch you have used at networking events. No need for wordsmiths.

You're doing a lot of pitching already, you just don't realise it.

Digital PR

We also now have a plethora of emerging online news and entertainment outlets and their performance statistics are hugely impressive in terms of readership and social sharing.

This new Digital Media is hungry for stories. They need to pump content out by the minute, not just breakfast, lunch and tea time bulletins.

You have a story to tell, somewhere within you and/or your

business. By taking what your business does and finding a relevant news angle, or providing expert advice, you can easily bag yourself some space in this online content world for the mere price of some professional photography, some writing time and a few emails.

A good example of this is my school friend and designer Sandra L O'Hara. She wanted some exposure for her new business *BlueMeadow Bridal* so I advised her to use the current news story of the downturn in funding for the local Arts Sector.

We pitched the angle that the downturn was encouraging young women like her to become "Creative Entrepreneurs." One press release. One professional photo in her studio. 10 emails.

Sandra wrote a small advice piece for entrepreneurs and 'hey presto', multiple online articles and social media mentions achieved.

These digital outlets aside, even if old-school press relations remains a staple of PR work; how and where we interact with those journalists is moving online.

Outside a handful of experienced correspondents for traditional elite publications like the Financial or New York Times, journalist roles change so often now that the days of building relationships are almost gone. Anyone can find a journalist or news desk, pitch them and quite easily achieve media coverage, if their story is news worthy (more on that later).

And that means PR is now accessible to the masses.

The good news is that a lot of the groundwork is done simply by doing it yourself. You don't need to teach an agency all about who you are, what you do or what you want to achieve. You don't have to spend a meeting taking part in flip chart activities like "If your company was a car, what brand would it be?"

You know your business better than anyone. So let's get started.

Who To Contact and Where?

1. We will start from the assumption that you know your audience - be they customer, service user, potential member. If you're selling to them then you know their demographics. You know what drives them. And you should know where to find them; whether they read a newspaper or an online news site, and which ones. Every news outlet will have a Twitter profile and may even have different profiles for each section (such as fashion or technology) if they are particularly large. They will also, invariably, follow and Retweet every journalist who writes for them. And don't forget your own industry trade press and the places you go to for advice as a business person. List them all.

2. Almost all journalists now use Twitter and many welcome being contacted there via Direct Message. Even if they don't, they will often advertise their work email address within their Twitter bio. Failing this, most news websites will now have very detailed contact pages incorporating the names of each editor and writer as well as email addresses and even Twitter handles. You can of

course try their generic newsdesk@ or editor@ email addresses but they will be swamped with emails, sporadically checked and so your story may be overlooked there.

3. You need to use online channels like Twitter and their plethora of old article links and personal information on timelines, to find out who is responsible in each industry area at each news outlet, get their contact details, see what stories they like and pitch yours to them. Make a list of every journalist relevant to your business or add them to a Twitter List for reference later.

4. Speaking of Twitter Lists, other peoples' lists are also a great place to find contacts without doing all the data mining research yourself. Think of a business like yours, only bigger. I follow a few UK and American consultants who do what I do - including blogging and selling books - but on a bigger scale. They will inevitably have Twitter Lists for industry journalists to pitch to. In the same way that I have made my own media lists, divided up into UK, Ireland and Beyond categories.

5. Once you have a list of contacts, you're ready to pitch. Depending on your time scales, it would be a good idea to follow these journalists for a while and start engaging with them; liking their stories and commenting on industry issues that you feel knowledgeable or passionate about - topics you have something to contribute to, in order to show up on their radar. But don't worry if you don't have time. Plenty of out-of-the-blue media pitches are successful even by experienced PR professionals who have had no choice but to cold contact a new journalist. If the story is good, they won't care if they don't know your name.

In my experience they want information, not new friends.

6. Don't forget freelancers! It may be harder to get a feel for their content themes but with variety comes opportunity. An in-house reporter can only pitch your story to their editor once. A freelancer can spin it a multitude of ways for a multitude of media outlets, thus making themselves more money. And making you more coverage.

> **Top Tip:** Anewstip.com is a separate search engine to find journalists who have covered specific topics or brands online. Again, most will have their email addresses in their Twitter bios. And Media.info is a good UK source for basic contact details in mainstream media outlets too.

If as a last resort you are trying to guess the email address of a journalist because you know their name and the bit that comes after the @ symbol then you can use mailtester.com to quickly check which of the email address variations is valid at that domain host (e.g. lross @acupoflee.com / leanne.ross @acupoflee.com / etc).

What To Say?

The most shocking revelation to businesses is the fact that the question of "what is newsworthy?" is a bigger problem than who to contact in the media. This is the part you're normally paying for in terms of skill when you outsource your PR - the creativity and experience to know quickly what stories and angles will work for your business.

But there are some basic ideas that don't take long to learn:

- Announcing something new (especially if it's a "first")
- A new product/service, moving into new markets, exporting or contract deals, new architect designs for developments...
- Job creations, big name appointments, special guests
- Contract wins
- Investment/revamps/rebrands
- Award wins
- Starting construction work ("cutting the sod")
- Completion of construction work
- Grand opening/unveiling
- Sneak peak photos inside buildings/shops/events before launch
- Events (before and after)
- Company milestones
- Anything with figures (business media love statistics) such as monetary figures, world firsts and record breaking headlines
- Campaign launches, charity partnerships, sponsorships
- Anniversaries - especially if the industry/prices/products have changed with time (even just since last year)

If your company is really new, like just-out-of-the-egg-new, then you're in luck.

Your first foray into media relations is your best opportunity to gain coverage. That's because the media loves the novelty of new ideas, new products and new faces in order to keep their content fresh and their audiences interested.

It also explains why most people will see the best results from their initial first month's retainer work with a PR agency or consultant, and why it will then wax and wane depending on news opportunities from within and outside your business (or depending on the attention you're getting from your chosen PR supplier).

However, launching a completely new brand or reinventing an existing one can be difficult if you don't have the big budgets that global companies do. But there are ways around it. You'll find more information on one of the more traditional PR tools for this - Desk Drops - in Chapter 5.

If you have enough budget however, a one-off stunt can gain maximum launch exposure, especially if you have primed the media in advance. This is because in the age of transparency we now need to be shown, not just told, how good a new product is. Launching a camera for example? You could drop yourself out of a plane to record how good the video quality is.

If you're into that sort of thing.

Can You Become Newsworthy?

If you don't have any news just now, it's quite easy to either create your own or newsjack (hijack an existing news story):

- Create survey results (Surveymonkey is a popular free tool for this) - just remember you need a minimum sample size of at least 500 or 2,000 if claiming to be representative of the general population
- Comment online - reply to journalists on Twitter who post links to articles that you have an opinion on or feel knowledgeable in
- Comment by phone - listen to the morning radio news programmes and call in if you have something to contribute
- Write an open letter on a topic for your website or submit it to the Editor's Letters page of a newspaper
- Submit a guest blog idea on a topic you can contribute to as an expert to a leading blog in your industry (again, they will list their pitch contact details on their sites)
- Ensure your own website blog content is not too sales-pitchy and more topical feature-style with how-to articles, and it might get picked up by media anyway (more on this in the Digital Communications section)
- Offer yourself as a candidate for business profiles in recruitment sections, business magazines and even the more casual "personality" sections of your local newspapers
- Keep looking for fresh angles on your business, what you do, what you know and how it fits with what is happening in the world today
- Be ready with stories for seasonal holidays, industry trends, celebrity events, popular culture and national "Days of the Year"
- As with the above, keep your creative juices flowing for

zeitgeist opportunities. A timely social media post tying in with a major sporting event or similar can garner press coverage as a result of the topic's popularity online
- Create your own infographics to display information and statistics - online media in particular love these - and free tools like infogr.am and Piktochart make it relatively easy to do yourself.

If you're thinking up a "PR stunt" for an existing product or service there's also lots of fun to be had, from changing your name (like Marmite did for the Queen's Jubilee - "Ma'mite") to making fun of your rivals (like when Pepsi dressed up as Coca-Cola for Halloween) or even inventing pretend products (such as Ben & Jerry's ice cream tub locks!) Most of these require simply a graphic design mock-up image and a press release. The changes/products rarely happen in real-life.

There are many more examples of story ideas to pitch when it comes to creating your own brand content (such as blog posts) and I cover much more on how to generate relevant, popular, ideas for free in the Blogging Chapter.

To make sure you tie your own plans in with wider media themes, some major media outlets, particularly magazines, will publish editorial calendars in their advertising sections like InStyle's one so you can plan ahead for the coming year and see the best time to pitch them when they're covering your topic or product area.

But the real trick is to learn to be creative with content that links in with what you do, without being an outright promotional pitch.

So if you want coverage for an app for parents, for example, you might think about broader lifestyle articles:

"Which pram is most likely to help you burn calories in the park?"

Or you could run a survey for interesting family articles around:

"Life lessons your pets will teach your children"
"Stay-at-home mums are XX% happier than working mums"
"How to raise a child and SAVE money"

Or you might want to look at seasonal ideas such as:

"The top 10 gifts for new dads this Christmas"

See what we're doing here? Not rocket science, is it?

Hyperlocal Content

Another heavily-used tactic in online PR is the idea of hyperlocal content.

It works really well with modern audiences because it cuts through the online noise to bring something very specific to the attention of a subset audience.

What it brings them is so highly engaging and relevant that they enjoy it and often share it too, helping this type of content enjoy a lot of online traction.

From the Buzzfeed-style "10 things you'll only know if you're from Belfast" to the listicle "Top 5 burger joints in Dublin" you will know hyperlocal content as soon as you see it, even if you didn't know the technical term for it.

Creating it is often simply a matter of tweaking what you've already got, and pitching it separately to local media, with local statistics, places or people highlighted within it.

Alternatively, you can simply create this type of content for your own blog or social media, perhaps only loosely related to your product or service, as a way to build a relationship with your local community.

To Press Release or Not To Press Release?

The press release celebrated its 100th birthday a decade ago in 2006, which marked the anniversary of the first news release about a derailed train in Atlantic City that killed 53 people. It was created and sent by Ivy Lee who is widely regarded as the founder of modern-day PR.

Don't fear the jargon, though. A press release is basically just an article; a story with an introduction, a middle and an end, a headline on top, a quote or two from the main characters thrown in. And contact details at the bottom if the reader wants to know more or ask a question. 1-2 pages max.

There has been a lot of discussion in the industry of late as to whether or not the press release is "dead". Most PR people argue that it remains a staple part of how they do business.

On a personal note, I don't like press releases because:

- It allows for lazy journalism among bloggers and media alike, and can result in verbatim articles copied and pasted (known as "Churnalism")
- This is a massive problem for your search engine optimisation efforts if it happens online because Google will penalise your website (put it lower on the search rankings) if content on your news web page is found duplicated verbatim elsewhere on the net
- They always sound boring and cheesy and include egotistical corporate quotes nobody believes.

OK I can't prove that last one, but I stand by it. I've written more CEO quotes in my time than I care to recall, sometimes for people I've never even met. And more often than not, they are not included in the eventual article when a good journalist decides to chop the release up and add their own slant to the story.

I can only speak for myself but, when given the freedom to choose how to pitch - i.e. not dictated to by a client or agency contractor - I've had some good feedback from journalists about my initial email pitches. And here is one that was referred to as "...perfect, can't tell you how nice it was to get a PR email that actually explained exactly what the story was and how it was relevant to me."

(Yes, those are quotation marks. Yes, I am smug about it).

The pitch, to a renowned Irish journalist, is copied below as an example. It was to launch an Irish waist training corset company.

As with all media relations, the bulk of work in preparing the media launch went into sourcing fashion and showbiz columnists and their contact details, as well as preparing separate feature article ideas for each depending on their locality and audience.

This was all new to me - the topic, the industry, the press contacts. So I was starting from scratch, in the same way that you, the business owner, would be.

The journalist didn't mind being contacted cold because the story was newsworthy and the pitch was succinct and personal to her.

She couldn't run the story in the end because they had used a similar feature just a month previously, and so although hugely topical, we had to source media outlets who hadn't yet jumped on the trend. But the home grown media enjoyed the local aspect enough to run the story.

Email Pitch

Good Morning XXXX,

I'm approaching you for your opinion on whether you think this could work as a feature piece?

Why it's newsworthy: According to Google, searches for "waist cinchers" and "waist training" have more than doubled in the last year, thanks in part to endorsements from celebrities, including Jessica Alba and Khloe Kardashian, who claim that these products are the secret to their toned physiques. And around the world, women are recording their journeys as they train their waists in photos posted to social media channels, including Instagram where 100,000's of photographs have used the hashtag #waisttraining.

The Irish Angle: Now, Ireland's very own Cinch Corsets have taken the updated lingerie item to the next level with high quality materials sourced from the other side of the world incorporating modern design technology.

Celebrity: Irish glamour model, Former Beauty Queen, TV presenter and newspaper columnist.

Material Available: Myth-Buster Article, Promotional Photographs of celebrity modelling the items, Behind-the-Scenes video link for online articles/social media.

I've included the full release below. Would love to know your thoughts.

Many thanks,
Leanne

Admittedly, I did include a press release pasted after this in the email (not as an attachment), but that's primarily because the client requested it. Undoubtedly the journalist would have needed further information to write a feature but that could be sent in a more generic media kit too.

As journalists' resources continue to reduce and their inbox unread items increase, to attract their attention you need to back up a press release with additional content. Modern pitches can contain embedded images, videos, sound bites and links to a company's website, blog or social media accounts. Some news outlets will also require any press releases to be Search Engine Optimised (keyword rich) for their digital channels.

Regardless of whether you decide to write a pitch email or you would prefer to just send a press release, it is best to have one prepared anyway as a journalist may ask for it when writing their story, for back-up information if nothing else.

Media Kit

Where the old meets the new in the world of press releases is the idea of a "Media Kit". This is basically a number of pages/materials that you keep together and send with pitches, or after a journalist has agreed to work with you, to give them deeper factual information about your company.

It's best to divide it into sections and keep it succinct, as you would in an investor pitch, with less fancy descriptive words and more simple facts.

A great one may look like this:

1. A short description of what your company does, where

you do it, when you started, and a couple of milestones so far
2. A few quotes from the owner/founder/investors
3. Some quotes from customers/users/case studies, if applicable
4. Links to professional images like logos, key staff headshots and product imagery or photos of services 'in action'
5. An overview of financial information or existing industry research that was used to found the company (bullet point form) so that a journalist can pepper their article with statistics
6. Links to any other relevant material, especially for inclusion online, such as SlideShare presentations or video footage.

Follow Up Calls

Once you've sent your pitch or press release, you wait a while, maybe you hear nothing. Then it's time for... the trauma of all PR graduate experience - the follow-up phone call - which remains, strangely, a staple of the industry.

Usually involving a hurried phone call to a journalist who isn't too pleased to be interrupted, and normally being told a lie in the vein of "just calling to check you received our press release" is the industry equivalent of a desperate ex partner with a drunken late night text message.

It's embarrassing, nobody likes being the caller or the receiver and it has never, in my experience, led to a story being picked up when it was originally overlooked.

By all means ask for feedback if your attempts are falling on deaf ears, but you'll be lucky to get it from overworked, under-resourced news desk reporters.

Most media, in Ireland at least, are friendly and will let you know they received your email and whether or not the story will work for them.

Sometimes they will even be kind enough to pass it on to a more relevant department for you.

Be patient. Not every opportunity will get picked up. PR profiling takes time and effort to build. Your first introduction to the media will not have been in vain.

Now, at least, they know who you are.

But whatever you do, do not become unavailable in the immediate aftermath of media contact! This is a real bug-bearer for many agencies when clients go AWOL or they're trapped in meetings the day after a pitch has been distributed.

I even had one client go on leave for a week after a business announcement, losing them valuable broadcast coverage and making the journalist very annoyed with me for wasting her time.

Once you offer yourself to the media you're on media time. If they want an interview with you they want it now, or more likely, they want it yesterday.

Keep your diary free, your phone on and be prepared to go live on radio in 10 minutes. Have your notes to hand, fuel in your car, charge in your phone battery.

If you let them down at this first hurdle, you risk damaging the relationship for good.

Finding Media Opportunities

Of course there is an easier way to piggyback news with your products or professional opinion, without all the creativity and the pitching.

While PR folk and people like you are feverishly trying to create and shape the news, journalists and editors have their own plans and story ideas. As they're writing them, the need arises for case studies, expert comment and analysis to strengthen their stories.

Although journalists may become very knowledgeable on a particular sector they specialise in, more often in modern news desks, journalists will be working across platforms and industries, often freelancing to a plethora of media outlets on anything from parenting to fashion, business to agriculture. They can't be expected to be experts in everything, so they will seek out experts when needed.

Experts just like you.

There are paid-for services you can sign up to which will find these call-outs for you and deliver them to your inbox. The UK one I personally tested - JournoRequests - was a low monthly cost and resulted in an expert piece on the Guardian Small Business advice section for my own business in the space of just one month.

The Return on Investment for that £25 was pretty good.

However, that success did require answering and sending information to four or five different journalist requests in order to achieve that one piece of coverage. It cost more in time than the monthly subscription, but it's worth much more in terms of coverage gained even if you just secure one success per month.

And it's cheaper than a PR retainer, to be fair.

There are also some free alternative media request delivery sites, with SourceBottle being my personal favourite, although it was initially based in Australia.

HARO (Help A Reporter Out) is the biggest, and undoubtedly most popular in America, but the time zone delay can make UK and Irish pitches less effective.

If you're bootstrapping the budgets, it doesn't mean you have to miss out. The requests are available for free if you care to look for them. Most of the aggregator sites mentioned above are pulling their information directly from... you guessed it, Twitter!

> **Top Tip:** Journalists and bloggers will use hashtags such as #JournoRequest and #PRrequest in public callouts. Searching these terms regularly will alert you not only to media opportunities, but to journalists that you may not otherwise have come across who are covering your industry.

Undoubtedly, within the replies to their requests, they will handover their email address for case studies and BOOM - your media list is growing by the day!

Contract-Out Content

At the end of this book I do give my pointers on outsourcing some or all of your PR and Digital Communications if you feel that your own attempts aren't gaining the results you want, or if you simply don't have the time to do it.

However, if it is only the writing that is your weak point, then you could simply outsource your content creation.

Many freelancer copywriters will have a lower hourly rate than PR agencies or consultants and, because they often have experience of media relations and Search Engine Optimisation (SEO), they can write more competently for traditional and digital media outlets, as well as knowing how to repurpose your content over a multitude of platforms.

Of all the resource-intensive tactics within this book, it is the writing, if anything, that should be outsourced for maximum effect. By all means let the intern do your contact research. Do the pitching yourself. But don't leave the writing to an amateur if they aren't very good. Content will become the front-facing shop window of your business and what goes online stays online!

A Word of Warning

Editorial coverage is something the PR industry has worked for years to sway, direct, even sometimes control, but it isn't advertising and you don't have final say over the outcome.

Once you engage with the media, you can't dictate the angle that is taken, which elements (if any) of your business are included, or how big or small your eventual coverage is.

You can of course correct mistakes, spelling errors and untruths.

The trick is to ensure that your message is embedded firmly in your media relations pitch. From your job title, to your back story, somewhere within your three-line soundbite quote; however small the message is, you are still building awareness and gaining credibility.

Simply inputting a line at the end of a press release that states what your business does probably won't ever be included, because it is too obviously a sales message.

But if you are seen in the right places, commenting on relevant topics, or merely becoming a more recognisable name and face in either your local media landscape or your specific niche online community, you will be doing exactly what any PR professional would do for you - slowly, strategically, and much more cheaply!

Search Engine Optimisation

You'll see I've already mentioned SEO briefly and it will be referred to numerous times throughout this book, especially in the Digital Communications tactics in Section 2.

Hopefully you've at least heard of it. I know it's complicated. Even I don't claim to be an expert, but you need a basic understanding if the reasons behind some of the activities I propose are to make business sense to you.

I would recommend reading up on the topic, if only to appreciate the highly skilled discipline in some areas like Pay Per Click (PPC) advertising - which you really should outsource - but also to comfort you with how much of it is plain and simple.

So how does it work?

Search engines like Google, Yahoo or Bing, basically flaunt themselves to us as being the controllers and providers of all that is useful and wonderful online. That is why we love them - they find the best answers to our questions.

But the internet is cluttered by people (like us) trying to scramble our way to the top of the search rankings, by creating bucket loads of (not always the most useful) content.

It is in the search engine's best interest then to trawl through all this content to find and feed their users the most up-to-date, relevant, useful web pages on any given topic, so that we keep coming back. So they can keep making money from advertisers.

For that reason, search engines employ secretive ways and means (technically called 'algorithms') of teaching their robots to judge the content online and therefore ranking it appropriately, based on relevance and popularity, into an ordered list of search results.

When looking for something, most of us don't make it passed the first page of results. So that's where you need to be. Preferably near the top.

Why do I mention SEO in the media relations section?

Well the biggest problem for most new businesses is that the top slots on search engine results for their target keywords will already be filled by existing competitors. And their content will most likely be heavily optimised having spent years gaining social shares, links from media and therefore, achieving higher ranking by the search engine judges. Your content in comparison will take time (and money) to challenge that position.

Without the budget to pump into SEO efforts with a Digital Marketing agency, the main tactic employed to boost online ranking is called "ranking by proxy" achieved via…online press coverage. PR.

This is when a journalist covering your story online uses your target keyword in the article headline (headlines often make up the page title of the article and page title inclusion remains one of the key on page factors considered by Google.)

Likewise, if you can get the journalist to include a hyperlink back to your own content within the article, it too will help you gain inbound links for your website. This is another key on page factor for Google.

However you will find that many online media outlets will not include follow links within their articles. So you need to work around that, ensuring your articles quote your name, your business or product name, and other industry keywords together. Luckily in this instance, Google recently announced that mere mentions would be used to calculate website rank, not just hyperlinks.

And the social media links from people sharing your article will still benefit you too.

In the end though, the single greatest thing you can do to aid your SEO is simply and consistently create good online content for your customers.

But fear not, I'll teach you the bits you need to at least understand, before you outsource, in Section 2!

2 IMAGERY

"A picture tells a thousand words. That's never been more important than online, where we want to consume the whole story in just a few seconds."

"A picture tells a thousand words" was apparently first used by, ironically, a journalist. The expression appeared in a 1911 newspaper article quoting editor Arthur Brisbane who was discussing journalism and publicity.

It makes sense of course. When processing multiple sources of communication and digesting complex data, our brains do that all the more quickly with images than large chunks of text.

The tactic of imagery has never been more helpful than in our modern world where we are literally harassed from all sides by a constant stream of communication messages. We flick, or scroll, passed it a lot. But a good image can stop us in our tracks.

With that in mind, professional photography is the one area of PR that any agency worth their salt will encourage, nay harass, you to invest in. Without it, press coverage is almost impossible to secure.

But there are still ways to save money.

And even a few tricks that are free...

Portraits and Products

First impressions will always be important but now that we conduct so many of our initial interactions online, virtual personal branding has become as important as the handshake once was in introducing yourself to the world.

Once people know you, showcasing your product with pictures (particularly moving imagery like video), instead of words, is the primary sales weapon you have at your disposal.

Professional business photography then is an opportunity to portray a brand image to potential customers who aren't just researching what you do. They are just as interested in who the people behind it are.

In business we spend a lot of money on branding across logos, websites, literature, packaging and premises. Is the photographic representation of you and the product or service you sell, really the place to scrimp on branding?
Probably not.

If you intend to spend time promoting yourself as the face of your business and an industry expert to the media, then you will need a professional photograph.

I invested in my own first professional headshots last year because my regular guest articles and event appearances required it, and for two hours of my time and a mere 2-figure sum, it has more than earned it's keep across my social and business channels.

Make sure to find a photographer whose portfolio fits with your vision when it comes to your business and "brand you."

Press Photo Calls

A photo call is basically a staged stunt created to represent the news story, giving photo desk editors eye-catching images for their newspapers rather than using stock images or boring 'line-of-suits' corporate photographs.

For many of us in PR we know through experience that sometimes that single press photo is what we must pin all our hopes of digital and traditional media traction on.

The image is key to media coverage. Who is in it, the colours/lighting/positioning/editing – all of which hinges on a great photographer.

A good photo can also improve coverage chances by bagging you some Picture Desk space and a short caption even if there isn't room to be found (or made) for your full story. Or in the case where you have something to promote but not enough detail to fill a press release.

Picture desk email addresses will be available on news websites in the same way journalist contact details are. They will expect to be sent a high-resolution image (or Dropbox link or similar) and a caption outlining the who, what and where of the story. A couple of sentences maximum should avoid important information being edited out.

Press photography can go wrong of course. A quick Google search for "worst PR photo calls" will give you a flavour. The easiest way around this is to hire the services of an experienced press photographer. Start to look at the names credited in newspapers or magazines under great photos that have caught your eye, or ask people in your industry for recommendations.

Even a quick call to a media outlet or Picture Editor and they will happily tell you who they enjoy receiving good images from (and who to avoid like the Plague).

If you still believe 'Peter from down the corridor' and his new Canon can do the job, you're in for a disappointment.

Press Photo Tips

- Get outdoors (weather permitting)
- Where possible, use props
- Failing props, big letters/numbers will do (usually made of foam which is a firm prop favourite in the industry). Or helium balloons, for similar reasons
- No props? Use people. Line them out on the ground in shapes, make them jump in the air; bodies are props too
- Enthuse as much action, angle and meaning as possible
- Include a politician or local personality in the line-up if applicable
- Showcase landscape, vehicles or buildings in the backdrop, especially if it's a story about construction (get the suits to wear hard hats!)
- Use post-photography editing to remove blemishes or add effects
- They say never work with children or animals, but it will almost always pay off in terms of press coverage
- Practice and hone your caption writing - it should be a sentence or two that can cover who is in the photo, where they are and why (i.e. the main headlines from your press story) while also flowing well when read and ensuring all parties involved have been accredited.

All of these ideas will require a good press photographer to catch light, reflection, glare and shadows and come equipped with their own experience of what works or proposing creative ideas they've had success with before. So invest wisely.

In some cases, an event may be newsworthy enough to warrant inviting the media outlet's own photographer. Bear in mind they may only have one or two and so your pitch will need to be good.

A simple invite, like the one below, sent to Picture Desks or Editors, offering them to send a photographer to capture something visual in action such as a grand unveiling, a special guest or a fun event like a World Record attempt can work, as long as it's impressive and visual.

Media Invite

Who: is involved
What: is happening (make it snappy and intriguing)
Where: exact address - state name of person who will meet the media first and where they will be
When: date and time
Why: context, news angle, why it's important, what will make it worth photographing?
Media Permissions: any guests available for interview on what topics and at what times, if children are involved they will need to have signed parental permission, if surrounding landscape or buildings have given permission to be filmed also, etc.

We would love to see you there and encourage you to book a slot in advance if you require significant filming/interviews without other media present.

Picture Editors will usually confirm if they plan to send a

photographer or film crew but breaking news can change plans in an instant so you should always book your own photographer as a back-up to ensure you can get coverage afterwards if the media photographers don't make it.

If they do turn up, take note of their name and which publication they work for, so you can buy the newspapers or visit their websites the following day, to check for coverage. They won't automatically send it to you.

Remember this isn't advertising, they owe you nothing.

Social & Digital Imagery

Imagery used online is a bit more illustrative and personality-fuelled than the corporate shots we expect to see in printed press, trade magazines or on company websites.

And the meme styles of text-on-images for humour is one of the most obvious ways to gain viral traction online today, because people want to be entertained as much as informed.

But you don't need a graphic designer in-house to create the basics.

Canva is a website used by most digital communicators these days because it is free, quick and easy to use, and extremely professional looking in terms of the final product.

There are freemium options within it of course, including the offer to purchase more or better stock imagery and templates, but you can upload your own images into templates already measured perfectly to size (for Facebook headers and Twitter posts).

The sheer scale of editing available in terms of fonts and colours allows for complete personalisation so often no one will know you have used the service to create your images.

You can then upload the finished images to your website, social media accounts, blog posts, use them within presentations, even download high resolution copies for printing.

You may not have the time or ability to teach yourself Photoshop, but you can master Canva in a very short space of time and triple your design output efforts.

Top Tip: Placeit.net is a great free tool to insert your logo, book cover, or other marketing images onto template computer and smartphone screens, magazine stock images or promotional items like cups and t-shirts, without the need for advanced editing skills.

Stock Imagery

If for some reason you need to use stock imagery to bolster your own growing library, or as a basis for your Canva creations, there are some really good websites offering free stock imagery that doesn't need to be credited.

Some of my favourite websites include Unsplash and Picjumbo. Pablo, a free tool owned by Buffer, is also widely used when you just want to create an aesthetic stand-out quote on a nice background to be used within presentations, blog posts or on social media channels.

Google search itself has also implemented an easy-to-use system for finding licence-free imagery, by showing a drop-down tab under their "images" search tab called "usage rights." In here, you can choose to only show search results where the images are 'labelled for reuse with modification.'

3 EVENTS

"The physical world hasn't lost out entirely to the digital one. Not least in our desire for real, human interaction."

From exhibitions to business breakfast briefings, lunchtime seminars to training events, evening networking to the age-old open day; the opportunities for PR and digital content continue with events...

Invite

Events remain a great way to give people a physical introduction to your business. Press releases work because journalists enjoy writing about new things. But in my experience of working with new companies, nothing can really sell what you do like the passion conveyed in your presence, the sound of your production line, the sticky note plans on your office wall.

For that reason, open days are a great PR tool, especially when so much digital media now utilises video footage as well as photos in their articles. Some media outlets actually have Video Journalists as a separate specialism on their staff list for such events.

Instead of just sending out a press release explaining your company or product, why not invite journalists to come and see it in action? This is a great sell for broadcast media, TV in particular, who rely heavily on atmosphere and images to give depth and meaning to a story.

Of course, the invite still needs to be newsworthy. To announce your own news or tie in with a topical issue.

Open days work really well with a notable visit, say by a local politician or leader, which is easily organised by sending a request for a visit to the relevant government department.

They will appreciate the good publicity as much as you will and will usually organise it to coincide with a bigger policy announcement - which guarantees you coverage!

Teach

In the modern market, it's no longer enough to tell people you're great at what you do.

You have to show them.

One of the reasons blogging is such a great business tool is that it proves to potential customers that you really know your stuff. If you're selling to a local market, an even more targeted way to do this is by hosting your own informative seminars and briefings.

Technical service firms have done this for years, particularly in areas such as law and insurance. They can instil enough fear in their audience with tales of what can go wrong when the uneducated try to do the job themselves, followed by comforting the audience with success stories of where they have saved the day for their clients.

A lot of Digital Marketing agencies now do this, investing the cost of quirky venues and finger food, inviting local businesses to attend, free of charge, to get an informed introduction to a service that is perhaps specific to them, or very technical. Anything that is hard to sell properly in a leaflet or on a website.

It works because the businesses now not only know who the service providers are, but they have started a face-to-face relationship with them (eradicating cold sales leads) and they will trust them more than a stranger to deliver that service as a supplier - based on what they've seen at the event.

None of the prep work will be wasted. The presentation used at the event is both pitch and public speaking practice. But it's also a way to create new content which you can then repurpose afterwards across your social channels, on places like SlideShare if it's a PowerPoint for example, or by uploading event photos/video to your social channels.

And the fact that you're even doing the event may be newsworthy to your local media, especially if you're linking it back to a topical issue, time of year or celebrity story.

Meet

Despite the major benefits of online networking (which I cover in Section 2) face-to-face networking remains a vital component of business development in the early days.

And indeed many of the most popular regional online meet-ups (such as the Twitter chat #BelfastHour) have become real-world events. Belfast Hour isn't organised by anyone in the digital sphere though. It was founded, and is still managed, by a local law firm. There's no reason why you can't create and host your own event, making it more relevant to you and boosting your profile at the same time.

Top Tips

- Partner where possible to share the load or, in the case of partnering with a charity or local venue, to share the benefits
- Use online ticketing services like Irish startup Get Invited which offer all the great services of traditional systems -

email list compilation, social media promotion and registration assistance - without charging the organiser a fee for free events
- Keep it simple. A lunchtime session, a quick presentation, a Q&A with a small panel of knowledgeable people - some tea and coffee, maybe. It doesn't have to be complicated, it just has to be worth the effort for your attendees as well as yourself
- To build a database list of interested people you email post-event, you could offer incentives in exchange for warm-lead follow-up, such as a small eBook of tips or a "business card raffle" where people enter with their card for the chance to win a free consultation or product. These entries, more than mere attendees, will be further down the sales funnel for your product/service.

Fundraising

"It's good to do good."

But more than that, partnering or supporting charitable causes is a two-way street of benefits.

Charities often have high-profile patrons, existing communications teams to conduct their Marketing and PR efforts, a committed group of public donors (who will extend their goodwill to corporate supporters) and an open ear from local media who understand the value of real human stories that charities bring them.

Fundraising events also offer a lot more in terms of creativity, public goodwill, and photo opportunities for local media coverage. But you don't have to create your own. You can sponsor all, or some product, at existing events like running or cycle races, children's days or record attempts. Even the local marathon has a banana sponsor at the finish line.

Or you can allow staff time out to volunteer with projects, on mentoring or befriending schemes. This creates more newsworthy hooks for you throughout the year, and more depth to your brand story.

All this positive local activity adds to your overall Corporate Social Responsibility - giving back to the community that sustains your business - which does't just improve business prospects and PR opportunities, but is also known to boost staff morale and increase your ability to recruit the best candidates and retain the best people.

Don't be shocked that there are selfish motivations to business goodwill.

I'm teaching you the art of spin, remember.

Virtual

Growing in popularity now among PR and Social Media Marketers alike, is the idea of the virtual event.

From "Twitter tastings" to conference live-blogging, the idea is to send everything the participant would need to them in advance - be it products to try or links to live streams - and then ensure they have the details to join in, whether it's through social channel handles, hashtags or password-encoded website links.

Then it's simply a matter of letting the engagement and conversation play out, as it would in real life, but online, in front of a bigger audience.

The key is to have a few confirmed participants, like bloggers or influencers, who will lead the charge and ensure there are no silences, which can be as awkward online as they are offline!

4 AWARDS

"Win or lose, the confidence to sell yourself is a reflection of the confidence you have in yourself."

Awards are relatively inexpensive for the profile return they yield, reaching a highly targeted group of industry peers and professionals, trade organisations and your potential customers.

And the subsequent credibility boosts your ability to speak as an expert in your field.

Of course there is work involved in applying, and that is what puts most people off entering. You have to find the relevant awards, complete the entries, pay a fee (sometimes) and then attend ceremonies if you're announced as a finalist.

But the bottom line is, awards will help your bottom line.

Finalist or winner, the credibility will help when tendering for business. Your profile will be boosted by media coverage and it will give you something newsworthy to create content around.

The good news is that once you complete a few applications and hone your answers, it's only the figures and project examples that need to be updated for future applications.

In fact, if you're doing any of the content work included in this book - such as blogging, social media marketing or media relations - you will have a backlog of written business examples each year ready and waiting to be copied and pasted in.

Win or Lose

I know we don't always win (I've lost myself) but there are many other business benefits to entering industry awards. You believe you're good or you wouldn't be charging for your product/service so back yourself. Make the commitment to prove how good you are, to say it publicly, to lead the charge for those you expect to also invest the same confidence in you.

The act of applying, often with limited word count, forces you to explain what you do concisely and evaluate your results effectively. This is an exercise you should be doing as part of your strategic business planning anyway (in fact most award entries end up looking very similar to business evaluation reports).

Many awards are free to enter and still bring with them exposure within your industry and outside it through social and media coverage, particularly if you are named as a finalist, but especially if you win.

Again, there's a skill in completing entries and again, it's a task often outsourced to someone like me. But the first one is usually the most time-consuming. After that, a lot of it is "copy and paste" and regular updating.

If you're going to be selling your product or service then the best practice is to become experienced in selling yourself!

Admittedly for reasons from resources (both manly and monetary) to availability of suitable examples of work, agencies and large corporations have tended to dominate award short lists.

But the tide is changing. Increasingly within PR for example, the voluntary sector is investing in its communications departments, bringing strategic expertise to the sector and, therefore, sector-specific examples to the judging table.

In-house professionals are now seeing the benefits of award entry outside those obvious to agencies (such as competitive edge when tendering) and citing boosts in staff morale, recognition of their departmental work at Board level and an enhanced pool of candidates when recruiting for new posts.

Even losing has a benefit as most awards panels will provide some feedback so you can build on what you've achieved so far and create a superior entry on the next attempt.

Profile Raising

Most award providers will do their own PR around the finalist announcements and results. This may include shortlist announcements and winner case studies and you could get mentions from it, but don't sit back and think that leaves you covered PR-wise.

Remember that they will be targeting their own industry and local/regional media as opposed to that which would benefit you individually. Don't be afraid to ask them for press information to help you write your story, as well as the appropriate logos or official photographs that were taken, and gain permission to try to get some media coverage for yourself.

The awarding body will be grateful for the additional coverage and the ability to advise you in advance as to their own brand guidelines.

What To Enter?

The first thing a PR agency would do for you is draw up a calendar of industry-relevant awards, in a basic table, including deadlines and any fees. They would use a simple Google search, so there's no reason why you can't do it yourself:

- Start by searching for industry awards linked to your main business focus, e.g. "industry + awards"
- Look at any awards operated by professional bodies (such as Institutes and Federations)
- Search your local business bodies like Chamber of Commerce
- Local banks, airlines, even Supermarkets and business magazines often run their own business or industry awards
- Then look further afield to regional bodies and European/International awards (bearing in mind the bigger the pool, the bigger the competition)
- If it's relevant, look to more specific business operation lines such as technology, design, digital, or logistics (if that's what you do)
- Even go so far as to look at specific role-based awards, from your Marketing efforts to your Receptionist (if you have one). There's an award for most things.

Top Tip: You can also find a generic list of Business Awards with annual deadlines on websites like The Awards Agency or Boost Marketing's Award List (which also offers an Awards Alert email service).

Form Filling

In every part of life we hate filling out forms.

Award entries can feel even more daunting because they tend to ask high-level questions like evaluating outcomes against objectives. The great thing is that the internet now enables us to access previous winner case studies, which are usually hosted on the award body websites. You will find much of the example language and ideas you need from these.

Alternatively, copywriters can charge a reasonable hourly rate and be well-versed in completing industry application forms. It could pay off dividends to get help with your first form and use it as a baseline for your future applications.

Below are snippets of an application focussing on results, for an award I won in 2012 (Best Not-for-Profit Communications). The full entry remains available on the CIPR website:

Specifically the communications objectives were to achieve:

1. An increase in referrals
2. An increase in service users
3. An increase in proactive media and stakeholder engagement

This work stream has succeeded all original objectives:

- Referrals increased by 46% (an additional 12,112 people)
- We saw more people than ever before take up their services – an increase of 32% with an additional 10,000 hours of service provided due to a rise in volunteers
- The organisational profile increased substantially with

sustained local and regional broadcast, print and online coverage achieved (with over 1 million Opportunities To See).

You can see clearly here that, aside from all the detail and examples that may have been explained within the application, the crux of it is the initial objectives/aims and the evaluation results that show those aims were met or exceeded.

There will be other areas of note sometimes, like overcoming challenges, inventing new things, doing traditional business in innovative ways. But for the most part, it is your ability to communicate your statistical achievements succinctly that is key.

Selling Yourself

As someone who has had to complete a form myself, not just for business awards, but for a personal award, no one appreciates as I do how gut-wrenchingly embarrassing it can be to sell yourself.

We're simply not wired to do it, in a world that worships modesty and demeans the fame-hungry and overtly confident.

But you have to remember that sitting quietly in the corner doing a good job can, and will, go unnoticed. You must put yourself out there and take the risk in order to gain the recognition you most likely deserve.

Win or lose, it will be worth it in the end.

5 DESK DROPS

"Your handwriting, the postman's delivery, a gift wrapped parcel - the personal touch feels special."

Building relationships with journalists and influencers is a way to get the word out about your products/services to more people through their engaged audiences that are much larger than the audience you're trying to grow.

Of course you can't build a relationship without first introducing yourself and "Desk Drops" have long been a staple of the PR industry for doing so among the media and bloggers.

My Desk Drop

When I started my own business, I created a Desk Drop for a mere £60 (plus postage) sent to all the local PR agencies in order to tell them I was now providing freelance subcontracting work.

The drop consisted of what was a wedding favour - individually wrapped tea bags branded "You're My Cup Of Tea" and a postcard with the famous (local author) C. S. Lewis quote: *"You can't get a cup of tea big enough or a book long enough to suit me."*

The idea was a play on words to my blog name and social handles (a Cup of Lee) which would then become my business name. I hand-wrote a personalised message on each postcard that I hoped the recipient would consider me when they were thinking over a tea break about how to meet ever-growing client demands with only their existing staff list.

It resulted in 8 meetings, 5 pieces of work, one ongoing subcontract project and referral to 2 clients with monthly retainers. As a tactic, it speaks for itself.

However, this idea can work across many industries and I've recently suggested to a photographer friend to do something similar; by sending cardboard cut-outs of popular PR props such as loudspeakers or speech bubbles, with a personalised not to encourage fun social media photos. It would show he really understands what PR staff need from a press photographer but to also stand out, within a reasonable budget, among a sea of pitch emails and printed leaflets. Creative, thoughtful and personalised always works best.

There are other cost-effective creative "twists" on existing PR practices that can get you on the desks, and in the minds of, potential customers and those who influence them through the media:

Alternative Press Release

This alternative press release example could be considered old fashioned now given the technological advancement passed memory sticks, but it's still a great idea which, strangely, wasn't copied as often as it could have been.

An image went viral in the media world when a UK PR agency sent a press release launching the "Charlie and the Chocolate Factory" musical to journalists on a USB stick that was shaped like a Wonka Bar.

Simple but effective.

So many press releases are emailed and lost in the crowd these days. To receive a "snail mail" package still excites us all a little. And when it's chocolate-shaped, fun and creative, it will more than likely garner some social media coverage.

Let Them Eat Cake

This one is sometimes considered a little cliché since everyone started doing it, but there's no denying the joy we feel when baked goods are delivered. The age of the exquisitely-crafted cupcake came... and it hasn't gone away. Just look at the annual national frenzy surrounding the "Great British Bake Off."

What we should remember here is that it's not just the design of the treats that's important, so much as the online influence of the recipient.

Everyone in the PR industry remembers the cheap and cheerful cupcakes sent to Stephen Fry to announce the release of the Muppets Movie in 2012, when one camera phone photo reached his Twitter audience of millions for the price of half a dozen iced buns.

It works well these days when it's personal. Irish company Chocolate Manor does this quite well in my opinion, with their personalised chocolate bars accompanied by heartfelt, handwritten notes. The bars are sold as corporate gifts or promotional items, so it makes complete sense to implement this very tactic in order to sell them to business customers.

Media outlets are also keen to utilise sweet treats and will often be seen sending ice cream trucks to advertising agencies to celebrate their audience figures (i.e. to promote themselves as an advertising platform to agencies who hold client budget purse strings!)

Wait a Minute Mr Postman

Like the press release idea or the cupcake deliveries, sending anything by post does feel that little bit more special. The sender will have gone to some effort (packing, researching addresses, booking couriers), perhaps substantial expense too, but it always elicits a little excitement to receive a surprise package when you're stuck at a desk all day.

However the media receive a fair amount of "desk drops" and a good proportion of them aren't great. Sure, free product is nice, sometimes even useful, but if journalists started talking about every free pair of socks or sample beauty product that landed through their letterbox, they wouldn't get any real work done.

So think carefully about what you invest in. Make it creative, fun or useful. Personalise the accompanying communications and encourage social sharing with your social names and any hashtags.

The gold lies in the initial idea.

Top Tip: If you're a press photographer, send some props. Own a lingerie brand? Send a branded tape measure. It can work on so many levels. Minimum cost, investment in time and genuine human effort. And that will always be rewarded with a sincere response if nothing else.

6 DIGITAL COMMUNICATIONS

"It's the same communication you've always done, just in a different place."

Digital Communications is everything else you do and say online that isn't explicitly media relations. It's that simple.

And creating good content may well bring media coverage to you, rather than you actively chasing it. This is the basis of the new concept of "Inbound PR" being bandied about the industry at the moment.

But forget the jargon.

All it means is that you create enough useful "stuff" online, from producing helpful articles on a blog to excelling at customer service on social media, and you will attract customers and journalists alike to you, rather than you having to seek them out.

Why do you need to?

Firstly, because you can't rely on media coverage alone. Traditional media coverage is still a challenge to achieve. For example in the tech sector, it was recently estimated that around 10 big companies accounted for more than 40% of tech press coverage. You can probably name those companies off the top of your head.

So already, media space for your little company is almost halved. Solution? Find other ways to communicate your message to the public...

Content Marketing

Content Marketing has become one of the most popular themes discussed in modern digital strategies of late, although it's been accused by some of being nothing more than the latest buzz word.

When you break it down, content is just "owned media", i.e. the posts, blogs, research, images, speeches, websites, videos, eBooks and other content a company creates. Content that you own.

Content Marketing is simply when you use that owned media in a cohesive plan which puts it on specific channels to target specific audiences and achieve a specific outcome, more often than not, through online channels, usually to convert fans to customers.

In that respect, Content Marketing is new in nothing more than name. It could be argued that the Content Marketing industry has been around for well over 100 years. The American agriculture company John Deere is often credited as the pioneer with their publication "The Furrow" which was originally printed in 1895!

Whatever you term it, as a process it is undoubtedly important. Optimising your websites and blogs, engaging meaningfully with audiences on social media, website link building and increasing your search engine rankings, and ultimately attracting people to your organisation because they believe in what you have to say, not just because you've asked them to buy from you/support you/etc.

It all builds brand credibility and loyalty which ultimately brings sales leads.

The Psychology of Content

Why do we love all those crazy viral links so much?

Well we know why we like the videos that make us laugh, or the stories that make us cry. Emotion connects us. It makes engaging in the virtual world that bit more real for us.

But in terms of branded content we're always talking about being useful as well as entertaining.

And useful works as well as entertainment because of the way the brain reacts when we learn something new.

It releases the happy hormone - dopamine.

And then the brain wants more of this rewarding loveliness and it makes you seek out more useful stuff.

And people who are looking to build their own profile online, perhaps to become an industry leader, benefit from curating and sharing useful information to help grow their own audience.

That's why practical advice is the type of content people love to share the most.

eCommerce

Nowadays, the new wave of digital technologies is transforming the front-end of businesses - the revenue generating end.

New digital innovations like cloud computing, ecommerce platforms, mobile internet services, big data and social media, are all radically changing the business landscape. In employing the technology, even small businesses can 'go global' from day one.

Today's path to purchase is evolving, meaning survival, before success, relies on keeping up with this technology.

Thankfully in Northern Ireland, our business community is thriving through technology, leaving us a litany of successful case studies to learn from:

Chain Reaction Cycles have become the poster boy of Irish e-retail, growing from a family-run shop in 1984 to become the world's leading online bike business.

Their online turnover now exceeds £170 million across 180 countries worldwide. Utilising the latest commerce platform technologies and digital marketing strategies, they managed to triple turnover between 2008 - 2012 with two thirds of the sales coming from outside the UK.

Uni Baggage started two decades later, in 2009 from Paul Stewart's student bedroom. It has since expanded into worldwide shipping, transporting more than 1,000 tonnes across 6 million miles.

The key to their approach is even more embedded digitally - an entirely virtual business. The key to their success lies in placing a resource and investment focus on digital advertising, content marketing and social media engagement with at least two blog posts and over 100 Twitter conversations every day.

Argento has grown to become the UK and Ireland's biggest retailer of designer brands like Pandora and Thomas Sabo. Founded in 1997 by Pete Boyle, the company now runs over 40 High Street jewellery stores with more than 300 staff. They may have announced an investment in physical stores in 2014, but part of that £1million was well spent on improving their website's functionality and Search Engine Optimisation.

Utility Bear, is the latest kid on the online block. Having spent many years selling successfully online through sales platforms like Amazon and eBay, the High Street menswear store decided to invest in its own new brand identity and online sales platform, improving its reach globally and investing in social and digital strategy, both paid and earned, to showcase their wares.

Make no mistake, your Digital Communications can convert fans to customers.

Now What?

With UX-optimised websites, ecommerce platforms and social channels people can find you online and purchase from you too. Now you need to shout about it so they know where you are among all your competitors. And that's where Digital Communications comes in.

From website content to SEO, blogs, email newsletters and social media management, it comes in many forms and is the next step in helping digital businesses reach their future audiences in a more cost-effective, precisely-targeted and easily-evaluated way than ever before.

You don't need a separate digital strategy, you just need to integrate your existing business goals and tactics into a plan that incorporates digital tools.

This just means thinking more broadly about how to apply digital and social elements to what you already do, rather than starting with digital tactics with no plan of what you want them to achieve.

7 SOCIAL MEDIA MARKETING

"Word of Mouth is now word of mouse - relationship building and influence move online."

Disclaimer: Social Media Marketing isn't a direct selling tool.

Oh, has no one told you that?

Well that's what the people selling it to you as a service know to be true.

What that means is that it will not always drive immediate sales to your website. In fact, direct email marketing and SEO continue to outperform social media in terms of link conversion. Sure social shares can help Search Engine Optimisation, but to what extent remains a mystery to anyone outside Google Head Office.

Instead, your efforts on social media are an attempt to build relationships. The platforms can help you develop a brand reputation, benefit from public endorsement or reviews, conduct customer service and eventually create brand advocates. This means that when the time comes to purchase, or people are in the mood for a spontaneous purchase, they choose you because your overall behaviour, brand and messaging has resonated with them.

Or because their friend rated you. And they saw it on Facebook.

If you create content that is valuable people will still recognise it is a sales tool, but if it's helpful or entertaining in some way then they will forgive you for it and allow your message into their news feeds.

With dedicated, quality content, you are creating a feeling, building a loyalty and cultivating an overall environment for selling that may just be that extra push a customer needs when they're at the point of purchase.

Scary Social Media

But social media is not the answer to all your communication problems. It isn't free for a start. It is a massive time commitment and time is money. It's also easy to get wrong. From mistakes that are instantly screen-grabbed and shared virally to merely spreading yourself too thin and appearing on all platforms half-heartedly, I can understand why some businesses are fearful of even dipping their toes in the social media sea.

Despite the worries, developing a strong social media presence is now really important for brand growth in an age of Social Commerce, with key networking channels like Facebook and Instagram working hard to develop their own purchase platforms, moving consumers away from traditional retail websites like eBay and Amazon.

Away from your website. Unless you're promoting it on social media too.

The impact of social influence is also increasing from the days of personal recommendations in traditional marketing to an environment where consumers are exposed to not just the purchase decisions, but the broader brand endorsements and feedback/reviews from their own family and friends.

The brand leaders in the field of online sales all offer something above and beyond product information and promotion on their social feeds. They deliver engaging content which aligns with their brand values. Some brands do this through education and advice (like Gucci's Little Black Book app) or cultural content and global community issues (such as Rolex's Pioneering Innovation projects).

Some brands add gravitas and a focus on competitive spirit with sponsorship, like the Grey Goose Toronto Film Festival. This type of value-added marketing relies on storytelling and social media provides the perfect platform for the two-way engagement stemming from it.

Sustained social media presence also provides the ability to monitor competitors and customers through social listening, virtually networking and learning what your customers want, where and when, in real-time.

Social media profiles now show up in search engine results too. All the major search engines are placing increased emphasis on social media channels because they tend to have regularly updated content, and often provide relevant results to people's questions. Websites like Google look for information that is topical, relevant, and useful to users, so if you're talking about trending topics and relevant content from the world outside your brand it can be hugely beneficial.

You see people don't use social media to shop. They use it to be informed, entertained or to simply socialise (hence the name!) so it is widely considered a bad place to go to sell things.

However recent industry research confirms that social media can influence retail sales: 40% of all social media users have purchased items online or in-store after sharing or "favouriting" them on Facebook or Twitter, according to research from Vision Critical.

So it should still form part of your overall audience communications.

If you are going to use Social Media Marketing as part of a sales strategy then there are some best practice guidelines to stick to:

1. LISTENING

Social media allows you to see what existing and potential customers are saying about your brand but also, about your competitors. Their behaviour in terms of engagement is there for public view. You can immediately analyse which of your messages are working and which aren't based on your own engagement, as well as researching what other content your customers like and using that to inform your own strategy.

You can then watch the performance of your main competitors to directly compare with your own. At its most basic level, if you see a competitor let a customer down on Twitter for example, you can swoop in and help them.

And if customers use your channels to complain, that's good! No, really. Because you can publicly show how great your customer service is, address untruths/myths and bring back customers you might otherwise have lost.

It's an epic PR opportunity.

Consumers will have the negative conversations anyway.

Make sure they don't take place not behind your back.

> **Top Tip:** FollowerWonk searches the bios of Twitter users to find influencers in your industry to follow and Google Alerts emailed to you will keep track of any news/blog mentions of you, your brand, or your keywords across the internet.

2. RELATIONSHIP BUILDING

If the key to selling and then retaining customers is relationships then social media offers the perfect platform to build them. You can interact, rather than "talk at". You can take on board feedback to make your products better. You can offer immediate customer service and you can show personality and draw people into a trusted, long-term relationship with your brand. They may also become advocates and share your message for you, working as a sort of communication amplifier.

As for your competitors? Well, not only should you be following them, you should be engaging with them. Like their posts, comment under their articles and even highlight their work by sharing it where appropriate. Why? Well that's where a large chunk of interested audience lie in wait to know about you. It's not about stealing followers. There's room enough for everyone.

For example, I follow a number of shopping centres online. I live near one, my son goes to school near another and I work with one. I'm allowed to do that. As a consumer, it varies my choice. If they all decide to engage in some friendly banter between each other, it'll only endear me more to all three of them.

> **Top Tip:** Tweetdeck is a good free tool to manage Twitter discussions online and respond quickly to mentions and messages as you can watch multiple news feeds/message inboxes on the one page, as well as creating customer search feeds.

3. CALLS TO ACTION

Companies are understandably fearful of actively selling on social media in a bid to avoid looking desperate or pushy, thereby turning people away from their brand. This is true, however you still need consistent messages to convert visitors to sales leads and website click-throughs. How do you do it? By simultaneously remembering what your followers want from you and what you want from them. So in posts, give them both what you want to say and what they want to hear.

Incorporate your links, promotions and messages with your fun statuses, newsworthy posts or topical debates. Offer your fans and followers exclusive promotions and competitions and encourage sharing. Ask them to get involved in the two-way relationship by doing something for you in return.

> **Top Tip:** LeadPages isn't free but it's widely regarded as one of the best sales funnel conversion tools for websites and blogs. A cheaper alternative is to use the Call To Action buttons on Facebook or Twitter Cards (which populate the form securely once the person clicks the button) or by putting your web link in the descriptions of Pinterest images.

4. INVEST

Social media is often referred to as "free marketing." There is an element of truth to this in that the channels themselves are free to use and most of the content needed to populate them can be taken from your existing content online.

However, you must remember that you are building your online channel on someone else's land – you don't own it, they do. At any time they could take it away. So invest in your own content platforms at the same time, be it a blog or your website. Ultimately, these social channels need to make a profit just like you and so they hinder how far your messages can reach.

Facebook is the prime example, massively reducing how many of your own fans can see your content unless you pay to boost your posts. So invest in quality, knowledgeable Digital Marketers to skilfully target sponsored posts and adverts when you need to spread your message further.

Remember too, the human investment of time required to post content across channels and think about automation tools to minimise that effort, such as scheduling systems like Buffer, Hootsuite or the free Tweetdeck for Twitter (and Facebook's own post schedule facility, which is also free).

Top Tip: You can set up your own Facebook or Twitter ads through their publishing platforms but you risk wasting your limited budget if you use it as an expensive practice session.

5. ANALYSE

So many organisations using social media assume they need to pay a Digital Marketing agency to come in and analyse the statistics in order to better target their communications.

But in most circumstances the social channels will offer you all the evaluation you need, for free. Between Facebook and Twitter analytics alone you can find out who your audience is, their age, gender, location, when they're online and which pieces of your content they like so you can do more of that and less of what they don't like.

Don't be afraid of analytics, you can't break anything by going in and having a look (I focus on evaluation tools in the last section of this book).

Top Tip: Facebook's own Page Insights are really good once you get used to them. Likewise, Twitter's analytics are improving. External tools like Nuzzel are good for telling you the most shared pieces of content among your network so you can use that to inform your own content strategy.

---

6. PERSONALITY

This can be tricky whether it's because of the corporate nature of your business or perhaps because you deal with a serious subject or a vulnerable societal group, like children for example.

This is why it's important to have people who deeply know your ethos managing your social media.

A great work-around is to diversify your social accounts.

If you want to be very serious because you engage with political representatives, government departments, funders or regulators, then your CEO or a senior representative should be online and interacting with those targets, preferably on Twitter.

Retailers also increasingly separate their customer service accounts from their main accounts, especially on Twitter, so as to not clog their profiles with negativity.

It frees up your main channels to give the public a more feel-good, jargon-free idea of what you do. But more than understanding what you do, you want them to grow to like you.

So show your staff working hard or celebrating a birthday with some cake at tea break. Show your guests at an event. Show your suppliers giving the thumbs up as they deliver stock or show your customers out and about with your product. It takes only a smartphone camera and the mindset of always being on the lookout for good content.

As long as you have some sort of content plan in place, you needn't fear overrunning your channels with humour and losing your core messages. After all, people want to be engaged with, not talked at.

Today's social media users are savvy and they know when they're being constantly advertised to, as opposed to being encouraged to build a relationship with you.

With that in mind it's important to involve your customers in your business to build a community: ask questions, run polls, engage in issues that people are talking about (if relevant to your business) and reply to every single comment, share or message.

I cringe when I see public complaints and reviews go unanswered. Many companies will tell me they took an issue offline and answered the person privately. That's all well and good. But the hundreds or thousands of other people who visit your page don't know that. They see you ignoring a customer. And that is bad.

So always look at your social feeds from a stranger's point of view and be sure to engage everyone, nice or otherwise, and ensure you're seen to do it publicly as well as privately.

And don't leave your feeds as a re-hash of existing content from other sites, although it is advisable to include the odd useful or relevant links from other sources to inform and entertain your audience. Sites like Scoop.it are good for delivering topical content to your inbox for this kind of content curation.

You have to create your own meaningful content, too. It needs to be a mix of relevant news, events, human interest stories, fun and the odd blatant promotion.

> **Top Tip:** Create a basic content calendar like the one in the next chapter a few months in advance, to keep your social media content strategically mixed and ensure you are organised enough to stay consistent and relevant to your audience.

Beware Being "Cool"

A backlash against companies using slang on social media was inevitable really. Brands started off being timid and shy on social channels, too risk-averse to immerse themselves fully.

Now the pendulum has swung the other way and many companies feel the pressure to be "more funny", "more controversial" and "more down with the kids" than their competitors to gain any cut-through.

For some brands a strategy of fast, direct, comedic posts works really well with their target market.

The problem with this uber-modern strategy comes when the language, tone and imagery just doesn't quite fit with who you are, what you stand for, what you sell, or the value base of the people you're hoping to convert to customers.

If you don't sell to teenagers, don't talk like one. Simple.

These pitfalls can be easily avoided if you spend more time focussing on who YOU are and less time trying to be what everyone else is, or thinks is cool.

Inevitably, if you judge the internal voice right, then the external voice will feel authentic and you will reach the people for whom it really resonates, because ultimately they are the only ones you will benefit from connecting with anyway.

Social Media for B2C

You don't pick your channels based on what sounds popular in the media or which one is easiest to update. For example, Vine videos might sound too technical and time-consuming but if you want to market your services to young people you'll get more engagement there than the time you may waste tweeting to an eternally low number of Twitter followers, for whom your message is lost in their constantly updated timelines.

Likewise if your customers are on Snapchat but you don't know what it is or how to use it, you'd be better pumping time into learning it than updating a barren Facebook Page.

So what consumers are you trying to talk to?

The demographic that tends to appear on Twitter - tech users - is different from that on Facebook, which is sort of "the everyman." Instagram is more of a niche market. Fashion brands, for example, are successful across all these channels because they know how to segment their messaging, so they're able to talk to different key interests. They use each one in a slightly different way.

There are so many channels online offering people different ways to engage with both their personal networks and brands. Look for where your potential customers will be. I can guarantee you they won't be everywhere. More than likely they will favour 3-4 channels which they will use in a hierarchy system.

For example, currently mine would be: Twitter, Facebook, Pinterest, LinkedIn. In that order.

Focus your energy into making one or two of your audience's favourite channels the best representation of your brand and feel confident that by ignoring the rest, you are not losing customers, but rather you have lost the risk of spreading yourself too thin and ultimately damaging your public image and customer service.

Channel Focus: Instagram

Instagram is Business-to-Consumer (B2C) marketers' go-to social medium because of the beautiful imagery, blogger influence and magazine style appeal. But Instagram hasn't made it easy for brands trying to sell their products. The platform doesn't currently allow for any sort of direct commerce which makes it hard to track purchases it has influenced. However, it does boast a highly engaged audience of more than 300 million people.

Instagram has a 100% organic reach (unlike Facebook who charge for promoted posts to reach organic fans) so every post can be seen in every follower's news feed (although they threaten to change this soon, since Facebook bought them over.) It also boasts 15x more engagement than Facebook, so views have a better chance of converting into likes, comments or shares.

It can be a struggle to consistently promote products visually in an engaging way to the high glossy standard now expected so the best way to promote a brand on Instagram is to think about how the products fit into a larger "experience" or lifestyle, enabling the posting of related content rather than a stream of product images.

More engaging content like Geolocation (tagging specific places) and Gamification (turning fan engagement into a game such as competitions to search for photos, upload their own photos and videos, etc.) can increase audience interaction on what is essentially a magazine-style viewing channel.

Channel Focus: Pinterest

Like Instagram, Pinterest is hugely popular because of the photographic nature of the channel. People enjoy browsing beautiful imagery and Pinterest allows them to store it onto boards and share it with their own networks.

But the channel is much more useful than basic awareness raising to brands. In fact Pinterest is becoming a massive driver of website traffic (thanks to the embedded links in each image) as well as allowing brands to become useful - tapping into the "how-to" culture on the channel with DIY, tips and tricks, recipes and fitness workouts - and then allowing users to become the word-of-mouse marketers for the brands, endorsing and publicising their content.

Competitions, storytelling/themed boards and image-based

informative content are the best strategies for getting the most out of this channel.

Channel Focus: Facebook

Facebook has the direct customer service response and targeting tools to follow up the emotional draw of the visual channels.

Unfortunately on Facebook these days, content is only king if you've got the ad budget to back it up. Advertising aside, Facebook is still the largest driver of overall traffic compared to other social media sites, and it still yields results. For this reason it remains the most popular choice for brands across many sectors.

The key to an effective Facebook strategy is one that provides shareable content as opposed to a heavy focus on selling, which turns fans off the content (and lower engagement leads to Facebook showing less of your content in their news feeds).

Channel Focus: Twitter

Twitter success relies on a brand following - and being followed - by the right people rather than broadcasting to a mass market. Posting regular, informative updates, sharing news and photos, responding to anyone mentioning the brand as soon as possible and looking out for the latest trending topics among a target audience are the main result-yielding tactics.

Twitter is less about broadcasting messages and is more of a two-way conversation. If someone on Twitter mentions a brand in a tweet they can respond in real time. Twitter chats can be used to drive high levels of awareness among targeted audiences, too.

A good strategy also includes promoting content from popular external blogs and sources. For users, this creates an association with brands and influencers that have already built a reputation.

Social listening is as useful on this channel as social broadcasting. You can even see what other people are saying about your competition by searching their brand name and any hashtags they use regularly.

Channel Focus: Snapchat

Snapchat is massively popular among younger demographics (mostly 13-24 year olds) because of the live video aspect of the "snaps" and the fact that the content disappears.

It's equally popular with brands, not only to reach this audience, but because the counters make metrics such as views and screenshots easy to measure.

Behind-the-scenes event coverage, preview/sneak-peak snippets, flash sale announcements and scavenger hunt type competitions work particularly well for consumer brands on the channel.

This is one network where businesses need to be prepared to have an extrovert personality and take risks - you need to be fast and memorable to stand out; it's supposed to be fun!

Channel Focus: YouTube

On 23rd April 2005, a three-man start-up made history when they posted an 18 second clip of co-founder Jawed Karim in front of the elephants at San Diego Zoo.

Fast forward a decade and the video-sharing site is the third most-visited globally, and is now the second largest search engine in the world.

As a learning platform, how-to tutorials of many different kinds (but mostly beauty and hair) have become the staple of user consumption. In fact, in the decade since its inception, over 5 billion hours of beauty tutorials alone have been uploaded. The phenomenon has made millions of pounds for, and global stars of, many a bedroom-broadcaster.

One of the most famous – Zoella – speaks to over 7 million subscribers. In the five years since she started her channel she has created her own make-up range and a novel that outsold J. K. Rowling's debut for first-week sales.

But YouTube is also hugely beneficial for online PR.

PR is about two-way communication. Whether it's traditional media, social media or digital, it has always been the job of PR to promote positive brand awareness, responding to conversations about it, learning from it, and moving it forward.

Online videos took off for precisely this reason – there is nothing more personal in online communications than having an actual human talking to you. When it comes to "YouTubers" or "vloggers", what marks them apart from traditional broadcasters is their ability to connect with their audiences.

They can interact with them, learn about them (through their stats and comments), monitor what they like and give them more of it.

Likewise, audiences can connect with their idols like never before through this medium, asking questions, making requests, publicly commenting, or just simply giving a thumbs up or down. All of this material, added to a video featuring your product, is going to be substantially more powerful than any news article or written review ever could be.

Modern audiences need to feel in control of the media they consume, absorbing messages on their own terms. This signals a major shift in dominance from traditional broadcasters.

5 Benefits of YouTube for PR:

1. Communication – at its most basic level, the channel allows you to communicate a brand message to a global audience. There are localised YouTube options too. You can add subtitles or you can use language conversion to ensure no audience segment is left out.
2. Crisis – the speed with which you can broadcast a message through YouTube, as well as the human element of video messaging, lends itself perfectly to

crisis management, allowing brands to be both fast and quoted exactly.
3. Awareness – the reach of this free channel is worldwide, offering a new approach to building brand awareness of products, services and brand personality. The space is most expertly used by those who are creative and engaging enough to gain a dedicated audience or achieve the highly desirable social shares.
4. Campaigning – political and non-profit brands can potentially leverage the power of video and viral trends with limited budgets. Many successful examples across election campaigns, natural disasters and public uprisings offered the public 'un-edited', immediate, Citizen Journalism. The human case study element is especially fruitful for charitable causes where people respond to calls to action, a sense of urgency and human stories.
5. Sales – video allows for the age old "show don't tell" sales mantra. By showcasing a product in an engaging way, you're more likely to convert website visitors to customers. And videos embedded on websites even help to bring those visitors in the first place, with video ranking on the first page of Google much faster than traditional SEO.

The most important aspect in all modern public relations activity is measurement and YouTube's analytics allow for tracking user statistics, engagement, shares, feedback and conversions through to websites and sales.

YouTube content is also consumed over a much longer timescale and is easier to find among the archives than other social content.

While global brands start their own production companies most smaller brands haven't even touched the surface of the potential they have to engage existing and potential advocates through visual content and branded channels.

User Generated Content

A mainstay of modern content and social marketing strategies involves encouraging brand advocates, customers and the public to get involved in their own content creation - that will hopefully be positive enough for you to use it.

Like the media, brands are not gatekeepers anymore. They don't control online conversations about their products or services, the audiences do.

With peer-led endorsements being the most powerful sales tool on social media, brands can work to encourage a positive message from brand advocates. And they really should work on it.

Because the psychology of social proof tells us that people are automatically drawn to things they know their peers already trust. There are numerous ways to promote User Generated Content (UGC) on social media, with competitions forming the basis of the most popular campaigns.

But some companies are fully utilising the opportunities afforded by technology, from gaming brands like Minecraft teaching young people how to make YouTube videos, to apps like IKEA's that let you virtually test furniture in your home before you buy it.

Even if it's as simple as asking customers to show off their product in a post with a hashtag, asking for feedback or reviews, there will still be benefit in their content, however small at the beginning.

> **Top Tip:** Simply take a customer quote, putting it on top of a professional image of your product with your logo (using a free design app like Canva, for example) to create a piece of repurposed UGC that you can use across your social channels.

Just remember to keep the hoops people have to jump through to a minimum (this may include technical know-how!) and recognise that without creativity and the fun-factor, there would need to be something in it for them - be it a competition prize or a promotion code - to ensure the two-way benefit is met.

Social Media for B2B

Despite the lack of immediacy and direct referrals compared to Business-to-Consumer, social media is increasingly forming part of the Business-to-Business (B2B) marketing mix, as a tool to influence sales targets.

At the same time, many B2B companies have found out the hard way that simply being present on social media isn't enough. If you want to raise awareness and increase impressions for the brand on social media, it's absolutely crucial to plan a content strategy.

The goal is to have the brand seen by the customers/clients that will eventually be approached. Social media users are far more likely to purchase a product or service if they have some pre-awareness of the brand.

And brands can give potential business partners something more through social media. People turn to sites like LinkedIn, Twitter, and Facebook not just to interact with others, but also to read the news, track the markets and keep up with the latest developments in their fields of expertise — in short, they turn to social media to learn from other users.

This means you can position a brand as a valued contributor of information, and in doing so bolster brand visibility among potential clients.

Another advantage of promoting industry content on social media is the increased visibility for a company among its stakeholders such as professional associations, industry watchdogs and news outlets.

A good rule of thumb is to post one-third industry articles, one-third shares from other sources, and one-third company news or insights.

Best practice is to take the most interesting quote or statistic from an article and post that, along with the link and the Twitter handles of those referenced in the article. In this way, the people mentioned in your post will see it, and hopefully share it with their audience. (Also check for relevant hashtags related to the topic and include those).

The informality of social media also makes it an ideal place to build a relationship with potential clients. The trick is to find where your potential base are interacting (LinkedIn groups, Twitter chats, etc.) and become a part of those forums.

When you finally do approach them with a sales pitch, your presence on social media will have given them an idea of your brand and the services you provide. That puts you at a huge advantage over a cold contact.

Channel Focus: LinkedIn

LinkedIn isn't simply an online CV website. In fact its a very powerful professional networking tool, allowing for both personal pages and company pages.

Regularly posting updates and articles ensures an active and engaging feed for page visitors and contacts. LinkedIn has its own powerful content publishing platform too. This allows for the repurposing of content from elsewhere because it isn't yet included in search results and therefore duplication of content won't (as yet) harm your website's SEO. And if you are chosen to feature in their PULSE news round-up to all users, website visits can skyrocket.

Joining relevant group discussions is a great tactic. These groups vary in size, but it's best to join ones with between 200-1,000 members. Smaller groups won't have the influence but your voice might get drowned out in the bigger groups. Ultimately pick a group that you know you can add value to.

As you join and interact with groups, you may identify an opportunity for a new niche group to be formed. When you become the owner and moderator of your group, you gain leadership and recognition in the industry. Position yourself authoritatively and not in a sales way.

Monitor Competitors

Social media listening is a good way to keep track of public-facing information competitors share with their followers - especially if your target audiences overlap. Since two brands may be chasing the same leads, it's important to be aware of your competition's value proposition. Tuning into their social media channels is a good way to determine the areas of expertise competitors are highlighting with the content they share, and see how you compare.

It's also helpful to keep an eye out for any mentions of competitors' brand names - their missed opportunity to connect can be your chance to gain a customer. It can also highlight any recurring themes in customer issues in the industry.

And Finally... The Intern

If I've heard it once I've heard it a thousand times: *"We're getting a student in to run the social media stuff."*

You're going to let a teenager who is paid minimum wage (if they're paid at all), who knows nothing of your values, business strategy or corporate voice, to be the public-face of your business?

Good luck with that.

I'm not being unfair here, to students or businesses. I realise that Social Media Marketing is resource-intensive (it's why I end up being hired to do it). And I'm not trying to say that you have to have superhuman mental powers to do it (quite the opposite, I know some very able students with a natural flair that experience can't buy).

But as the boss, you need to be clever about how you spread your resources and still ensure accuracy of message while protecting your reputation. Who would you trust to attend a high-value business meeting in your place? Only those people should be communicating publicly for you.

My advice is to take said student, or volunteer or receptionist, and make it their job to plan and schedule, i.e. they go around teams physically or virtually (by email), find out what everyone is doing, plan some post ideas, research the linked accounts you could include in your posts and possibly even schedule the week's posts in advance. But always go in and check before it goes live.

Or you can explain to your solicitor why you didn't have the time when you enter your first Crisis Communications viral storm.

Simply find one channel best suited to your business, where your target audience predominantly is, learn how to use it, build an audience, curate good content and become an expert there, before you move on and risk overwhelming yourself.

(But do go and create an account on every channel for your brand name and logo, even if it lies dormant, just incase you 'make it big' and find you're unable to get the username you want when you branch out into new channels!)

8 BLOGGING FOR BUSINESS

"Blogging is simply talking about what you know and love so that consumers will grow to know and love you too."

Blogging sounds like hard work, and it can be to begin with, for those who haven't done it before (which explains why it's often outsourced to people like me).

But with free tools like WordPress or even the new Notes feature on Facebook allowing for microblogging, it's never been easier to become an expert publisher in your industry.

It's that old "show, don't tell" thing again. Blogging allows you to show you know your product, your service or your customers inside out, while offering them much more than just the initial transaction.

The benefits of content creation, rather than just curation, for online consumers are becoming increasingly well documented. Hubspot reviewed data recently from 5,000 online businesses and found that 85% had increased website traffic from content creation within just 7 months.

Content is obviously important for Search Engine Optimisation (SEO) and helping your website to rank higher when people search for terms relevant to you, because with content, your website will boast two qualities your competitors won't – regular fresh content, and quality content that answers people's queries/keyword search terms which will encourage others to link to and share it.

Another important aspect of SEO benefits from content creation is the fact that it helps your website rank for more specific, longer phrases that people might search for (known as "long-tail keywords") which, helpfully, can attract less competition from other brands than shorter keywords.

So, for example, I might want to appear in the first page of search results for the term "PR" but that's going to be pretty competitive.

However if I write lots of advice articles (as I do) then I might start ranking for topics related to what I sell, which also attract less competition. Say something like "PR for startups" or "social media for ecommerce".

Content helps with two of the three main elements of SEO - relevance and authority (i.e. how well you answer the search question and how trusted your answer is by audiences). The other element - technology - is something your web designer needs to work on (things like mobile-readability, page loading times, UX, etc.)

But being able to work on two out of three all by yourself ain't bad!

Don't know what to write about? That's OK. Luckily, finding out what people want to know in your industry is free:

What To Blog?

For example, if you sell shoes – use Google's auto-complete function to find out the most popular questions and then answer them. Type in "Shoes for" and Google will provide you with a list like:

- Shoes for women
- Shoes for men
- Shoes for kids
- Shoes for the gym

These are your first four article themes.

You can work even smarter with AnswerThePublic, a website that pulls the answers to your search terms together on one page for you. This is more interesting than simply search terms because it gives you the questions people are asking around your topic using typical question phrases (the 6W's - who, what, where, when, why, which, plus 'are' and 'how').

Questions, reworded, often make the best blog headlines - which are also vital to catching an audience's attention in a crowded online marketplace.

So as I write a blog about the PR industry, if I take only 1 question from a few of the sections, I get article headline inspiration like:

1. How PR Works
2. Why PR is Important
3. What PR Companies Do
4. PR Where to Start
5. PR When You Need It

Using these insights to inform relevant blog content will improve it's visibility, share-ability and therefore your audience growth and subsequent website hits.

Data Mining

Top Tip: Use online tools like Buzzsumo to find out what the most shared (popular) content online is, relevant to your sector, product or keywords for your website.

It's also a good idea to visit Buzzfeed - a global phenomenon in terms of online viral content (and annoyingly to some in the serious journalism world, the purveyors of all things "click-bait"). Searching their site for your keywords will bring up a host of popular online articles from their own writers as well as brand publishers, who you can 'borrow' ideas from.

Likewise following online forums like Reddit, where the public debate topics and vote their favourite content up the rankings, offers great insight into what people are currently enjoying online if you search for your specific product, industry or related themes.

Here, you will also find popular questions or requests for information among subreddits related to your industry which could spark an idea for your own branded content in reply. You could then submit it to Reddit yourself and it may garner shares from there.

Getting used to a community like Reddit will help you learn what kinds of content do well and you'll be following in the footsteps of some of the major online publishers, like the Daily Mail, Unilad and Buzzfeed, who have all run stories they found on community posts.

Well, why reinvent the wheel?

As with the "what is newsworthy?" section for press releases in Chapter 1, there are generic content themes that remain guaranteed good ideas, depending on whether they will work for what you do/want to say and obviously, which ones you feel most comfortable producing:

- Lists ("listicles" instead of articles) given our much-reduced modern day attention span. Works particularly well if it's "hyperlocal" e.g. The Top 10 Places To Eat in Belfast
- Case studies from customers, suppliers or partners
- Demo videos or How-To articles
- Testimonials
- Other User Generated Content (like encouraging customer photos with a product using a hashtag) which you then republish on your own feeds
- Frequently Asked Questions (FAQs) with answers
- Interviews with industry people or Behind-The-Scenes with your staff
- Offering guest posts from other people/brands who may have something useful to say to your customers
- As with press releases, any kind of company news (see Chapter 1) can be turned into repurposed content across your channels
- Customer newsletters can also be adapted into blog posts
- Your personal journey or the company back story
- Industry news and your opinion on topical issues
- Round up articles of successes, or failures, what you've learned, "What Not To-Do" lists, etc.
- Short templates or guides through to longer eBooks and white papers, if relevant to what you do (like what I've done with this book, because that's what I sell)

- Podcasts, live chats/Q&As or live streaming - works well at conferences or events
- Infographics with statistics, facts and quotes
- Photographs from events, awards, photo calls, etc.
- Humorous "memes"
- Running polls, surveys or quizzes through Facebook/Twitter themselves, using SurveyMonkey or using free tools like Qzzr
- Running competitions, using apps like WooBox
- Courses, webinars, online training - much more time intensive to produce but if applicable to your business they can be very lucrative
- Repurposing any reports you've created, uploading presentations you've given to Slideshare for social sharing, and then explaining the learning behind it.

You can also utilise basic Google searches to bring you back content ideas in your industry by using a "search operator" (like the * symbol) in between terms.

So for example I can search for "How to * PR" and it will give me lots of results, by replacing * with appropriate phrases. Results like "how to do your own PR", "how to generate good PR", "how to get a job in PR" and "how to combine PR and inbound marketing."

Top Tip: A Google search for "magazine + PR" or whatever industry you're in, you can find all the relevant industry titles and have a look through their old content for topic inspiration.

Blog posts are an element of what you will have heard referred to as Content Marketing and it's basically PR for SEO. But remember to ultimately write for humans, not the SEO algorithm robots. If people like your content it will be rewarded.

There are some great examples of companies who have led the way in reforming themselves into brand publishers, such as Cisco and Nissan, as well as the recent success of online retailer ASOS.com's magazine and content offering online which is challenging big name fashion magazines.

You don't have to become a content machine, but if you want to taste a small bite of their success, it isn't as hard as it looks to have a go at your own branded content.

The thing to remember is that it's not all centred around selling your product or service. Instead, it's about looking at your customer journey and providing engaging and useful content at every stage for potential customers, so that they build an awareness of and trust in you.

Technology

Everything you need to start blogging is available for free, or at low cost. Both on your existing websites, and on notable blogging platforms. The time investment, in trial and error, is all it takes.

Or if you really don't rate your writing skills, a copywriter won't cost the earth.

Rather than take you through blog setup, which you can find advice on in lots of places online, I wanted to break down the practical benefits of business blogging by using my own experience.

My Blogging Journey

My blog has been running for almost three years.

I originally started for two reasons: to create an online portfolio of content work and to build experience in using Wordpress which is increasingly used by companies as the platform base for their websites.

In the beginning I blogged more frequently (back then it was a few times a week) but the posts were shorter. In the last year I reduced this to one post per week, of a longer length with more detail, more images (appropriately tagged for Google search referencing) and more varied in topic and theme.

My publication rates are lower, yet my visitor numbers are higher.

It must be because the social media following is growing, I hear you cry!

Not exactly…

I don't have tens of thousands of social followers. And most of the industry leaders who do have clearly purchased fake accounts (it's easy to spot this because the number of likes, comments or shares they get will only be in the low hundreds compared to their fan figures).

Granted I do promote blog posts regularly on my social channels, including numerous links to the last post at various times of the day – to catch different audiences – as well as posting links to what I was writing about this time a year ago.

Despite all this social promotion, the daily Google Search referrers to my blog ALWAYS outnumber those who follow me on social media, by an average of 10-to-1.

Blogging for SEO

So Twitter will bring me one reader, Google will bring me 10.

Added to this, I may only blog once a week, but I welcome new readers every day.

Anywhere between 50 and 100 visitors a day will arrive because they were searching for content I had written about. And Google was showing them my website within the first few results, because I've proved I know what I'm talking about.

I think that's pretty impressive for a blog that is very niche, in terms of the topic but even more so, because it focuses on one tiny part of the world (Ireland). A world in which readers are arriving from all over it.

My blog is proof that consistently providing shareable, worthy content will benefit website SEO results. And adding Digital PR to the blogging mix can help your website even further.

When a journalist includes a link back in an online article for example, that's a signal to Google that the website is an expert in its field, that it is good quality and should be promoted. Likewise, when a key blogger tweets a link to it, that's a signal to Google too. And when people share the social media posts onto their own profiles, that's more signals.

By accurately categorising your blog posts and tagging your images you can help search engines further. "Metadata" is a technical term you shouldn't be frightened of.

It is merely information on a webpage that is held almost unseen, to help search engines know what's on the page. You input this info as "tags" and "categories" when you write each post. They can be keywords, author names, brands mentioned or longer terms.

For this post Chapter for example, I would include tags like "Blogging for Business", "Content Marketing", "Brand Blogging", "Leanne Ross", "Wordpress" and "Talk Is Cheap."

You can also include helpful search tags in the ALT names of images you upload to your blog post (replacing spaces in between words with hyphens to help the Google robots crawl over the data). Use them, they will help bring people to your content when they search for images as well as information.

Another great way to repurpose content and boost SEO efforts is to create Slideshare presentations based on your articles. Presentations on Slideshare (now owned by LinkedIn) are usually made up of short-form bullet points from the full post, with images or video links. In the way you would do to present an overview of information through PowerPoint at a meeting, for example.

A presentation creates more content to share across your platforms, while also bringing the possibility of new website visitors from Slideshare and, if you embed the new presentation in the original post, it will rank higher on Google because your article now contains "media rich" content (not just text).

But ultimately, the idea is to create more opportunities for useful, engaging content for your audiences and that is always the key to getting a return on your blogging efforts.

> **Top Tip:** Use a free tool like Gammarly to spell check your writing. It will also notice repetition of words and recommend similar terms to replace them with (this can help you vary the keywords within your articles).

Blogging Return on Investment

So while I agree that blogging has lots of benefits for a brand/company, including giving you a voice and personality, creating content for your brand channels, positioning you as an expert in your field and increasing your website visitors...

The fact remains that if you are selling a product or service, campaigning to change attitudes or you're promoting something to increase public awareness, a consistently-published library of well-written, technically-linked branded blog posts will be doing this work for you even while you're not working. It will bring people to your website or your social media channels or wherever it is you have linked them to arrive, and then if you have put the work in to create a high-value piece of content, they may stick around to find out more.

Or contact you. As they often do me.

In fact just before writing this book I was contacted by a local company who were searching for someone to deliver 'Facebook for Customer Service' training to their maintenance teams.

The manager found me through a Twitter search. Specifically, she found an article I wrote entitled "10 Quick Fixes for your Social Media Accounts."

After reading it, she felt I knew what I was talking about and could deliver the solution she needed. Because I had proved it publicly.

Blogging as an industry professional has brought me countless opportunities to network, gain business contracts and just enjoy profile-raising events such as:

- Radio interviews on magazine discussion-type shows
- Podcast interviews to give business advice to startups

- MC at networking and training events
- Guest blog for other platforms including the member knowledge exchange platform of an eCommerce firm
- Attend some of our biggest digital events and conferences like Digital DNA, free of charge, as a guest blogger or speaker
- Write advice articles for the UK Blog Awards
- Create PR roundup articles for industry media platforms as far away as Australia (like Sourcebottle)
- Brought me numerous pieces of work from independent Digital and PR Practitioners with high-profile clients.

Other Benefits

Understanding bloggers is another reason why I encourage businesses to blog. When you feel the pressure to produce regular engaging content and you understand what makes different audiences tick, you become more aware of how important good, targeted relations are to the bloggers you could end up pitching to work with you (explained in more detail in the next chapter).

Your own experience of blogging, however basic or small, will endear bloggers to you and ensure that you are engaging with them from a place of mutual understanding and respect.

Content Calendars

The key to both blogging (or creating any type of content) and then promoting it among your sales messages on social media, is to plan.

And this can seem quite daunting when you haven't done it. Staring at a blank page is one of the most intimidating things you can do (trust me, I wrote this book!)

But as with everything else I've covered, it's very simple. And once you see it you may be loathe to pay someone else to do it.

My plans are simply a calendar in a spreadsheet or table - listing the months and dates (highlighting in yellow the weekends when social media audiences tend to be offline more often).

I then populate this with every key date I can find from the calendar - including global holidays if the brand operates worldwide - then moving on to entertainment and sporting events, through to funny "Days of the Year" that might be relevant and engaging.

After that, I input the blog articles we have planned that fit in with the seasons and themes, and then lastly we look at the brand's own messages that they want to get out, which are usually more sales-like in nature. So things like promotions, new product lines, staff announcements, awards or any of the other corporate news covered in Chapter 1.

Below is a snippet from a draft calendar for UtilityBear.com - a global etailer (online retailer) of designer underwear brands - for the first few months of 2016.

This suddenly makes the job of social media management and content creation much easier because you feel focussed and prepared.

Of course there will be other things to do online, like answer comments and messages from customers, research and engage with potential blogger/influencer partners, source media journalists, and jump at any opportunities to get involved with relevant trending topics or news items that arrive via email alerts.

But you can't plan for those.

At least this way, your channels will never be empty, and you won't have to worry about losing your focus or brand voice.

	Feb	Mar
1	Auckland Anniversary Day	St David's Day
2	BLOG: Valentine's Day Gift Guide	Dr Seuss Day
3	Product Alert	BLOG: Mother's Day Gift Guide
4	Thank a Mailman Day	
5		Product Alert
6	Lace Day	Mother's Day UK
7	Superbowl USA	
8	Chinese New Year	International Women's Day
9	Mardi Gras	
10		Day of Awesomeness
11	White Shirt Day	BLOG: Who invented underwear?
12	Deadpool Movie Release	
13		
14	Valentine's Day	Napping Day (DST)
15	Grammy Awards	
16	BLOG: Which style is right for me?	Product Alert
17		St Patrick's Day
18	Product Alert	
19		
20	BLOG: Swimwear Guide for Summer	UN International Day of Happiness
21		BLOG: Pyjamas or Loungewear?
22	New brand announcement	
23	BLOG: Best underwear for gym	Holi (Hindu Festival)

9 BLOGGER OUTREACH

"Influencers are the new gatekeepers; citizen journalism is where the modern audience goes to be informed and persuaded."

It has been argued that the mainstream media – the traditional gatekeepers of news – are becoming less important. So too, then, is the worth of the advertising slots they sell, and therefore so are the paid-for, hard-sell campaigns that the advertisers and marketers create to fill said slots.

Meanwhile social networking, with its abundance of bloggers and

Insta-famous influencers, is becoming more influential. But it can also be confusing for brands and difficult to control. The age-old maxim about the public needing trusted "influencers" to tell them what to buy and think is closer to the truth than it ever was.

The beauty of blogs is in their viral capabilities and the public-endorsed nature of them, which means bloggers can do the PR work for you.

Research

The best way to approach blogger outreach is to treat it exactly the same as you would media relations, because they are simply another type of media outlet.

Many bloggers will be part of groups of larger bloggers and can be found on Twitter communities such as Ireland's ITWBN (Into The West Blogger Network). And for the more business-savvy bloggers, they may be signed up and using blogger networks such as LiketoKnow.it (the Instagram montisation platform) to earn affiliate income from promoting products and brands.

Over on Twitter, searches for the most popular blogger terms like #bbloggers (beauty bloggers) #fbloggers (fashion bloggers) #lbloggers (lifestyle bloggers) and #pbloggers (parent bloggers) will instantly bring up lists of writers in each niche area.

Follower Wonk is a great tool for searching Twitter bios to find bloggers and influencers in your industry. As with media data mining, utilising Twitter Lists to scout the contacts made by competitors or brand leaders in your industry will save time.

> **Top Tip:** If you're operating globally you can "search smarter" using Google.ie (Ireland) or Google.fr (France) to find bloggers in certain countries and even try searching LinkedIn, a channel all too often ignored in blogger research.

Buzzsumo, as well as being a tool for finding popular content, has the dual benefit of highlighting the influencers creating the popular content in the first place, who may well be interested in working with you on similar content.

Twtrland now operated by Klear's free version software will monitor a Twitter account and give an overall influencer metric rating made up of average tweet score, popularity score (based on engagement) and responsiveness score (based on reply times) which is a good customer service measurement. It will also provide top level follower demographics (age and location).

The major tactic often overlooked (because it feels a bit like snooping and offends the ego) is to look to your competitors and particularly those who are further down the "company journey" than you. Who are they partnering with on Instagram? What articles are they posting links to on Twitter? Which influencer photos are they using on their Facebook page? And how well does it seem to be working for them?

Of course, many authentic bloggers won't want to work with competing brands, or may be locked into sponsorship contracts, but the exercise will give you a better feel for who is open to your products and services.

Testing

Once you've found your target partners, tools such as Majestic SEO or Chrome plugins like Moz will measure the link value or organic search value you would gain from a certain blog mentioning you. It does this by understanding metrics like Citation Flow and Trust Flow.

If you find a blog that gets a lot of shares, then this is a good way of measuring influence. And if their audience is relevant to your business, then you can potentially get sales out of those shares.

Ultimately you will have to decide what you need or want from the partnership with a blogger – be it domain authority and improved search rankings for your own website or social media following growth through their existing loyal fan base – and then test each influencer's value in these areas with the tools available.

Valuing the worth of their publicity before contacting them can require a bit more technical digging, however most of the professional bloggers will own a media kit or rate card, just like a media outlet would. This should include statistics about their social audience demographics, their website visitor numbers and results from any previous affiliate link partnerships where they can show direct website visit and sales from their posts to a brand's website. Even if they don't have this published online, feel free to ask for the information.

Essentially, you're looking at more than just the blogger's audience size. You're also judging their reputation within your industry as a trusted voice, as well as their ability to grow that same trust for brands they have worked for. So how much of their audience are they actually engaging with in conversation as part of the community they've built? And how much influence do their opinions have on the buying patterns of their followers?

Pitching

- All bloggers work differently and so their lead in times vary but, as a general rule, at least one month's notice would be required to work on basic content and photography
- Familiarise yourself with their blog, past content, topics and tone of voice, noting the types of comments and social shares they get
- Research popular content online through places like Buzzfeed and Buzzsumo for example, to come armed with one or two interesting ideas for the partnership
- Like journalists, bloggers are not analysts, they're storytellers. Tell them a good story about your brand/product
- Interact with them on social media channels before making the final approach
- Make the pitch personal by finding out and using their real name!

What I am told time and again by social influencers is that they desperately want to be pitched with fun, creative and engaging ideas for their blogs, for both informative or entertaining benefits it could bring to their audience base.

Yes some bloggers just want "free stuff" or money for posts. But so many are crying out for more than just free samples. Even if you don't have a concrete idea, engage with them anyway. Most of the bloggers I've ever spoken to are really clued-in business minds. They have a creative streak to rival any PR agency if given a good product/experience to work with.

Bloggers are like journalists in many ways, and one thing they have in common is that they don't like being sent generic press releases via blanket emails. Although traditional media websites are integrating video, pictures, and other multimedia content more frequently in their coverage, they're still well behind bloggers.

The web-only platform of a blog gives bloggers ample opportunity to integrate public relations content into their stories. So send them a content-rich media kit, just like you would a journalist.

Budget

One of the major stumbling blocks for a lot of brands when it comes to blogger engagement is their shock at the realisation that it does not come free of charge.

High profile bloggers have made (sometimes quite lucrative) careers from their platforms and online audience following. Some of this income is of course from advertising, but a lot of it will consist of paid promotion, brand endorsement and even small services like paid-for-posts on social media.

As with User Generated Content from customers, unless there is significant benefit for them in getting involved for free, more often than not you will need to pay for their participation.

Costs can vary wildly from £100 to several thousand pounds (even just for a single tweet), depending on the person's profile, the project and the work involved.

Bloggers are not "free labour" and considering they deliver quite significantly in coverage terms and online engagement, they rightly deserve a value attached to their time and work.

Researching them costs you in terms of time, too. Most brands and, indeed, social media managers, find it difficult to locate, assess and 'woo' every influencer in their industry or location. Even when you do find them, the most notable can be expensive to work with.

When all of that is outside your budget, the best strategy is to think "Macro Influencers." The pool of "Insta-famous" social celebs is bigger than the few blogger names that have crossed over to mainstream popular culture. A bigger pool means more fish, and competition lowers prices.

Looking to Macro Influencers with between 20-50,000 audience figures can still mean reaching an engaged fanbase but at a much lower cost. They are most often found on Instagram or YouTube but haven't yet reached a point where social media can replace their job salary.

These influencers can be more open to content that will benefit their channel, help or entertain their audiences or to products and services in lieu of payment, particularly if an affiliate promotional code is available for their fans to use.

And, as they aren't so recognisable, you run less risk of backlash from the public about "paying faces" to push your product.

Advertising Standards

Remember that if a blogger is paid to promote a product or publish a post, then they are required by Google to state clearly that the post has been sponsored AND add a no-follow code to the URL link out to your website or product to stop Search Engine Optimisation value being passed on when it has been bought, not earned.

If that isn't done they may penalise you for attempting to cheat the system.

Always check your regional Advertising Standards Authority guidance and discuss the topic with the blogger in the project planning stages, to ensure you work with one who is knowledgable and above board.

Say Thank You...

...for positive coverage or even just polite declines.

Like media relations, blogger relations is about relationship building and maintenance. Manners cost nothing. But the lack of them will cost you dearly in the long run.

10 EMAIL MARKETING

"Email may be an old marketing tactic, but it remains one of the strongest sales conversion tactics online."

Finding new customers is a far more expensive exercise than encouraging more sales from existing or previous customers.

Startups and small businesses can initially think that social media is the Panacea to their problems, however we know it takes a lot of time, resources and now (thanks to Facebook) advertising money to really grow an audience there and even then, it tends to benefit your brand awareness and customer service rather than converting sales.

The real converter lies in reaching an engaged audience directly by growing your own email database because email marketing is among the strongest conversion channels for brands.

Email is more a personal, business-like transactional, with less interruptions than social media. You might have less potential customers on your list than the millions using social media, but they're already warm leads, so your chances of conversion success are much higher.

Some estimates place email as much as 40x more effective at acquiring new customer leads than Facebook or Twitter links and 6x more likely to get click-through on links.

Regardless of the specific figures, the fact that how it performs can be tracked through analytics makes it easy to use, understand and improve for even the least tech-savvy among us.

Despite the fact that it is considered one of the "old" ways of marketing, email remains popular because people feel they have control over it, that it limits brands to cut out the spam and send only the most relevant information.

And it is, for the most part, advertising-free.

You achieve success with it by offering them personalised, relevant, quality content that is timely with clear calls to action and preferably exclusive promotions or discounts, previews or competitions.

Email Leads

As well as the emails you collect from customer orders or enquiries, you can gather email addresses from your social followers. Facebook offers a sign-up button option, or you can invest in high quality programmes that embed into your website and social channels such as LeadPages (albeit at a price!)

Or you can simply ask people to email entries to competitions. However you get them, start collecting them.

When you are ready to send an email campaign/newsletter, Mailchimp remains my favourite free tool for creating databases and then sending and evaluating the email campaigns. It is particularly good at making personalised templates optimised for mobile (which is very important).

Return on Investment

Email marketing is among the strongest conversion channels for brands and retailers, and encouraging social media followers or existing customers to register and provide their e-mail addresses can result in converting some of these people into e-mail subscribers and, therefore, future retained customers.

The returns can be large because email is such a cost-effective and time-effective tool to use.

Many of the systems like Mailchimp are free to use until your subscriber list is in the thousands (MadMimi is a relative newcomer but is particularly cost-effective for larger numbers of recipients).

They allow for pre-scheduling in advance and, with A/B split testing, you can send different messages to different segments of your subscribers to see which one is more effective.

Software can even automate a lot of your sales follow-up emails such as feedback requests, basket abandonment, or remarketing.

Best of all, email can provide in-depth analytics for direct measurement and evaluation.

Content

The obvious, and yet most under-utilised place to look for email content inspiration is to sign up to your competitor emails, especially those who are leading the way in your industry. They will have done all the research, A/B testing and evaluation before you. What they learned will be plain to see in the way they now do things.

This is important because different types of email work for different sectors. For example, tailored product emails based on past purchase can work really well for consumer product brands (e.g. "Leanne here are all the sale shoes in your size online now!")

But this won't work for a more serious service industry, where a news curation email or video how-to may be much more effective.

If you have the budget you can also research which email templates work for people in your industry. Email Insights collects emails and newsletters from thousands of services. For example, if you wanted to see all the emails someone who registered to eBay received over a year, they'll show you.

> **Top Tip:** Wavelength is a great tool by Mailchimp to help you discover other newsletters with a similar audience to yours. After finding them you could offer to exchange content with them or pay for sponsored posts on their newsletters, to reach their audiences.

Another great way to get engagement by email is to give away something for free and then ask for optional feedback. It's a basic reality of economics – when you give something for free, the receiver is much more likely to give something back. Promotional codes or discounts for referring friends, social media posting, or reviews all work well too.

Simply make sure to keep emails slick, uncluttered, with just a few links/products/calls to action and check that all links work correctly before sending.

And only send when you have something newsworthy to say. If not, there's no need to keep in touch for the sake of it.

Don't waste people's time in a time-poor world.

Headlines

Of course none of the content inside the email will work if you can't convince people to open the email in the first place, and that all starts with a good headline/subject line. It will need to lure people in, without over-promising or click-baiting, which could damage their future trust in you and might make them unsubscribe from your database completely.

Avoid landing in the spam/junk folder by not overusing punctation (like this!!!), avoiding ALL CAPITAL LETTERS, ensuring no spelling mistakes and just generally not looking too desperate.

Readers tend to open emails from their inbox using a hierarchy system of importance. From things that look important, then things that are obviously relevant to them right now, or things they are invested in in some way, through to things that simply interest or intrigue them with their mystery.

You can elicit these feelings by using broad themes like:

- News: Tell people about something that is happening or has just happened that they will want to know about or should know about
- Tips: As with all other online content useful "How to" advice is great, so long as you connect your solution to the person's current needs
- Offer: Give something compelling, like a promotion, competition, or preview, that the recipient won't want to miss out on

- Question: Ask something that a reader will answer "yes" to, or make a sort of mystery or riddle that they will feel compelled to find out the answer to.

The Legal Bit

Check with the information commission of each country you're operating in but, for the most part, simply remember the rule of "Opt-in". People on your email list should have chosen to be there, by proactively opting-in to receive communications.

You should then make it extremely easy for them to unsubscribe, or opt-out, should they wish to.

11 SOCIAL MEDIA NETWORKING

"Go where your audience is. Talk with them, not at them. And then grow your own audience."

It may not be PR, as such, but it is very much Communications and, nowadays, more often than not it is Digital Communications.

But just like networking in person, Social Media Networking is a time commitment and one you should measure the value of carefully and only commit time where you yield a return.

There are many opportunities to network, engage with customers or clients, learn of opportunities and simply become more known locally and globally, by engaging in free online discussions.

Twitter

Twitter chats can drive high levels of awareness, so seek out ones that are most relevant to your business and take one hour a week to get involved. They will all have their own hashtag (e.g. #BelfastHour) and often a profile managed by a business or organisation, taking place on set days at set times each week/month. A simple Google search will find relevant discussions for your sector (such as #PRchat #CommsChat or #RaganChat in the PR world).

Be wary of being too available online though, as you risk looking desperate for work, with little of it to do. Scheduling posts on social management sites like Buffer or Tweetdeck (a free option) are different of course and people will recognise that you aren't necessarily online at that time. However, this may also lead to your obvious promotional message being ignored among what is expected to be a live, engaging, genuine group conversation.

In terms of what to do once you get to the "virtual party", looking for ways to help people is usually the best policy. Come to the chats ready to answer questions, post links to helpful articles and promote other companies or brands you have found useful. Ask questions yourself if you have any.

Authentic Twitter engagement will grow your audience. However, the most important element of Twitter-marketing yourself is not how many followers you have, but how interested they are in what you have to say.

Widely regarded as "the cheat's game" is the systematic following of every person you come across in the hope they follow you back. Which they often will. It's old-fashioned Twitter etiquette.

The tactic results in people who have 50,000 followers because they follow 35,000, but who may only get on average 2 or 3 replies or likes on each of their posts. This would suggest they aren't getting an awful lot of value out of their audience.

> **Top Tip:** Some people may have purchased fake followers back before Twitter clamped down on the practice of robotically growing audiences. You can test the proportion of real followers a profile has with free tools like Twitter Audit.

Unless people who follow thousands of other users have a vast array of specific Twitter lists to engage with segmented audience groups, then Twitter is a numbers game to them, not a professional social network. You couldn't possibly manage a timeline with that amount of posters on it.

You don't want to be seen to do that. And you won't see much business benefit from it the next time you ask for help or try to sell something. Focus instead on attracting followers that actually care about and engage with your content. It's more beneficial to have 1,000 engaged followers than 100,000 followers to whom you are invisible.

LinkedIn

If your business is less consumer and more Business-to-Business in nature, then try LinkedIn. Join and engage in their relevant group discussions, comment under updates and articles (posting your own links if relevant) and even think about starting your own niche group and inviting participants.

When you become the owner and moderator of your own group, you gain leadership and recognition in the industry. Position yourself authoritatively and create a discussion space if you feel a new targeted group would be beneficial to your industry.

It's also a good idea to create your own content on LinkedIn's publishing platform. It's a powerful way to create leads and increase your influence among an engaged group of sector peers.

You can repurpose content from other blog articles for this (as currently, Google doesn't penalise your website for duplicate content found on LinkedIn articles). Another benefit is that, unlike Facebook, you don't have to pay to ensure your article appears on every one of your connection's news feeds. People also have the option to "follow" your posts and be notified every time you publish, even if they aren't yet connected to you.

Better still, if your article is chosen to appear on the Pulse highlighted posts platform, you have the potential to reach an audience of thousands. For free. It's also extremely easy to use and features (equally easy to use) analytics which are emailed to you.

Social Media Policy

So what about allowing other staff to network and profile-raise on behalf of the business?

Well there's nothing like the thought of allowing staff to run their own social media feeds to send shivers down the spines of management.

Aside from practical training in usage there's little left in your arsenal than the social media guidelines or corporate policy to protect you from potential disaster. But how useful are these guidelines?

As with most policies, it's often argued that guidelines are merely there to "cover the backs" of employers and organisations. As long as employees have read and signed them, they can't sue you if you sack them when they make a major boo-boo.

On the other hand, if written well, they can be quite useful in at least directing staff as to your brand tone of voice and alerting them to the most common of errors.

But what non-Marketing staff lack in specific communications knowledge, they more than make up for in on-the-ground information, customer case studies and just general personality of the brand that many of us lose the longer we've been removed from "the front line."

So getting them involved in some way across social media is a risk worth taking in my view. At least we have plenty of disasters to learn from. Like when HMV laid off employees, leaving one (the Community Manager) in charge of the corporate Twitter account. Followers got a blow-by-blow account of the mass re-structuring through tweets like "We're tweeting live from HR where we're all being fired! Exciting!" In just 20 minutes HMV's followers leapt from 61,500 to 73,350.

Stories like this make all businesses sweat. Profusely. But they also make us wiser as we navigate what is still a relatively new issue.

It's a balancing act. If companies assume too much control over digital channels then they lose what makes them appeal to the public – the fact that they're run by humans. Humans who are empathetic, funny and sometimes a little rude. But mostly, humans who are passionate about the brand they work for, one they're helping to grow every day.

As with face-to-face conversation, as long as people use common sense they can't go too far wrong.

Don't Automate!

This is my absolute pet hate.

I'm often left gobsmacked that marketers, people who would charge you to do this work for you, have Twitter profiles set up to automatically tweet their Facebook posts, use bots to share anything containing a chosen hashtag (no matter how random) and, worst of all, set up automatic tweets and messages to thank you for following or promote you as "the most engaged user this week."

Social Media Networking is exactly what it says - social. Networking.

It requires real people, being social and interacting in real time, with other real people, if it is to ever be successful.

Social Media Marketing may well allow for scheduled posts and announcements but in human-to-human networking, you will gain more meaningful relationships from doing what you can in real-time, with real-effort in just one hour, than a robot could do for you in a whole month.

What To Say?

It comes naturally to those of us in the habit of self-promotion and virtual networking, but I know how foreign a concept it is to business owners when they start out.

Here's a quick list of some things you could tweet or post on a LinkedIn group to help you get going:

- Tips to help customers or service/product users solve their problems
- Industry news you have come across that you liked, agree with or disagree with - start a conversation
- Links to videos or other materials that inspires you

- Wider business news in your local community or city
- Inspirational business quotes
- "Life hacks" or "business hacks" you've found to help your own day run more smoothly
- Charity work or fundraising yourself or friends/family
- Tips for starting or running a business
- Experiences outside of work such as family days, attractions, places you've travelled to
- Friendly reminders of important holidays relevant to your business (e.g. Mother's Day)
- Thanking someone for help or a shout out after meeting someone and feeling inspired
- Asking a question about your business, industry or issue of the day
- Ask for help; try asking your online community before you Google something!
- Share content from your favourite blogs or online media sites
- Congratulate others or celebrate your own business and personal milestones
- Check-in at stores, restaurants or any services and feeding back on your experience
- Share or start a poll
- Share links to other places you network online, such as other social media accounts, and ask people to join you there
- Referring to some of your favourite businesses and personal service companies from the hairdresser to the paper supplier!

12 EVALUATION

"You could be busy with lots of useless stuff…"

In fact that's been the biggest problem I've encountered over the years doing this job; being really busy and not being sure what I was achieving. It all starts with not knowing the "why" of the "how" in the first place.

Probably an odd place to put it, at the back of the book you've already read. But then again, we do traditionally complete evaluations at the end of an activity.

The thing is, you really need to design it at the beginning, because knowing what you're measuring will lead you to only do things that will bring you outcomes - i.e. the things you're trying to achieve/change and not risk wasting your time on things that may be nice or fun, but won't help your ultimate business goals.

So I can tell you lots of different aspects that can be measured. Some of them will be outputs, some will be outcomes, but not all will be relevant to you and your business.

Remember when picking from this shopping list to choose only elements that both can be achieved by you/your team and will benefit your business when accomplished.

PR Data as a Baseline

Data is the new buzzword in the industry and everyone wants to hire a "data scientist."

I hate spreadsheets as much as the next person but data doesn't have to be off-putting. It's just about trying to find the trends and patterns within the numbers.

Social Media Evaluation

Most social and digital channels come with their own built-in analytics tools, but it's knowing what to measure and how it correlates with your own business objectives that shows you the real return on investment.

So is your website receiving traffic from blogger/media articles or social media posts? Have your search engine rankings improved? Are people signing up to your email newsletter through a Facebook call to action button?

Many social analytics tools work in real-time, so if you can plan ahead and set up tracking before the campaign begins (and well before the report is due), it will be much easier to access the data you need later, e.g. accessing tweets that are more than a few days old is very expensive, and more difficult than collecting them in real time.

The main themes we measure across social media are message exposure, awareness raising, actual engagement with people and conversions to leads/sales.

To measure exposure/awareness raising we need to check to see how far the message is spreading by measuring elements like:

- Activity - number of posts across which channels
- Reach - brand mentions by other people
- Exposure - impressions on news feeds/timelines

To measure engagement we count and compare metrics such as:

- Likes/retweets/shares/comments/Pinterest repins/Instagram reposts/video views
- Comments and replies from other people
- Participants of Q&A chats/polls
- Use of hashtags

If the goal was to drive traffic to a website or convert to sales leads then we track things like:

- Website URL link shares
- Post clicks
- Conversions (e.g. email sign-ups, sales, etc.)
- Website traffic - unique visitors - and referral channels (where they came from)

Then you simply track the percentage increase/decrease of these metrics over time.

Top Tip: Use a service like Bit.ly to shorten your website links across social media so you can get an overall view of how often each message has been shared and clicked through across all social channels.

Twitter Analytics

Twitter offers overview statistics and graphs for things like:

- Tweets
- Impressions
- Profile visits
- Followers
- Other tweets linking to you
- Your top performing tweets and engagements (per month)

Tweets Section - will show specific post activity and performance link clicks, retweets and replies with percentage growth or decline. Each tweet can be drilled down for specific impressions and link click statistics.

Audience Section - will show basic demographic numbers and data for location, gender and interest topic as well as mobile data carrier. You can then compare your overall followers with your organic audience to see if you're reaching the people you need to.

Twitter Search Function - use the generic search bar with some tweaks to further define searches for mentions of brands, campaigns or links, e.g.:

- Monitor mentions: acupoflee @acupoflee acupoflee.com
- Monitor sentiment: acupoflee :) or :(symbols
- Monitor articles/blog posts: acupoflee "http"

Hashtag Reach

Tweetreach will run a free report on a profile or hashtag to measure both reach and impressions however it is limited to the first 100 tweets unless you purchase a full report.

Followthehashtag is another good free tool for this, although again it will only track back 7 days on the free version so constant evaluation through the cycle of a campaign is essential.

Back Tweets will also search archived tweets for mentions of either a username, a hashtag or a specific weblink

Facebook Analytics

Facebook measures (and compares over time for you) things like:

- Page Likes (fans)
- Fan demographics
- Page Reach (impressions on news feeds)
- Page Views (including tabs if applicable and external referrers like Google)
- Posts - audience activity - likes, comments, shares, times of day

Facebook also shows you the most popular types of content and most popular post from competitor brand pages if you choose to watch them (they won't know you're doing so).

Evaluating Digital PR and SEO

You can also take advantage of all the (mostly free) tools that the PR and Digital Communications people come equipped with in their toolbox:

Measuring Media Coverage

You can set up Google Alerts for online news links mentioning your company, and offline paid-for media monitoring services if relevant/necessary depending on how active your PR activity is.

Website Traffic

Google Analytics can seem daunting at first but the free service provides a wealth of information about your website traffic, where it comes from, how people use your site when they get there, where they bounce off and a multitude of other key data.

The behaviour flow charts will also help you see where visitors are first arriving (useful if you've set up a specific campaign landing page or promotional page) and then you can see how they flow through the site, spotting any potential difficulties that make them drop off before completing a sale for example or using the contact form.

You either need to set Google Analytics up for your website or ask your webmaster/designer if you paid one to create the website for you, as they may have done it or can input the code into each page for you.

The main metrics to look for are traffic numbers (especially unique visitors) and referral sites bringing people to you, which should also identify any social media channels.

And if new visitors are arriving through search results you can find out what keywords they were inputting to find you.

Link Clicks

Using Bit.ly to shorten your website links (as noted above) will allow you to track the clicks on those links, even if someone copies and pastes the link into their own posts, across channels and websites.

This is especially useful if they use those links in places you can't track, like messaging services for example (known as "Dark Social").

Search Queries

By signing up (free) to Google Adwords you can use the tools within it such as the keyword planner to give you search volume data.

The more expensive the conversion cost for the keyword, the more popular it is. That means more competition. You may try creating more content around less competitive keywords and checking the Google Analytics to see if you begin ranking for those terms.

You can also search popular content on Google Trends. If the traffic for a particular topic was high enough, Google Trends will allow for some generic search information that could be loosely linked back to social campaigns if a hashtag search spikes at the same time as a campaign is running online. But if there aren't enough results sometimes it can't calculate a graph.

Domain Authority

The MOZ Toolbar tool is one that is often used during blogger/ media research to test whether a website is considered respectable enough by Google to be of value to your website as a referrer.

But you can also use it to check the approximate Page Ranking and Domain Authority scores being given to your own site by Google. An increase over time should indicate your efforts are working.

Likewise, it will show you the external links, like online news articles for example, that are pointing to your site and helping you.

Customer Feedback

Running a campaign survey through SurveyMonkey or even a simple Twitter and Facebook poll for feedback will make your audience feel involved in the process and can yield interesting and useful data for your continued improvement.

Surveys are also a great way of measuring awareness raising or attitudinal change, if that's what your work was trying to achieve. Just remember to conduct the same before and after so you have a baseline for comparison.

Email Marketing

Statistics from your email/lead conversion provider or Call To Action button clicks from places like Facebook or within your email marketing mail shots will show how useful your content is.

Also, continued growth of sign-ups and less bounces and unsubscribe data is a positive sign the activity is working for your customers.

Influencer Engagement:

- Blogger promotion and affiliate sales links
- Competition entries
- Article shares, social media engagement and comments on blogger articles and social channels
- Bit.ly link tracking
- Hashtag measurement.

There are other measurement elements that may provide insight into the benefits (or negatives) of your Digital Communications and PR work. Measuring them will of course depend on what you were originally aiming to achieve in your objectives.

For example, not all activity objectives are outward-facing.

A company may conduct a PR-offensive not just to improve an external reputation, but for internal benefits. Data such as increased recruitment pools, staff retention or staff satisfaction survey result improvements may be appropriate metrics in this instance.

Likes Don't Pay the Bills

Vanity metrics. That's what the industry calls them.

It refers to when you measure things like a big digital audience as a success factor on its own, when in reality all it can bring you is a boost to your ego.

I've worked for companies myself whose sole aim of their social media work is to simply gain more Facebook Likes than their rivals in a neighbouring city.

When in actual fact having more Likes without them being engaged followers (i.e. people really interested in your content and liking and commenting on it) can actually have a negative affect on your Facebook Page performance, because it lowers the relative popularity of your content, which then lowers how often they show your stuff to your audience.

Concentrate on being useful, entertaining and relevant to your customers and potential customers and forget about being popular.

13 OUTSOURCING

"At some point it won't be worth your time…"

It's all very well teaching you the how, but eventually your problem will be the "when" or the "who." I still think the how information is helpful, because if you're going to pay someone else to do this work, you should know what you're paying them for.

As with anything, you expect the professionals you hire to know what they're doing. So how do you know that they know? Well they normally show you, with examples of their work or recommendations from clients.

In the past, websites and brochures were littered with client testimonials and quotes, links to previous examples of work and online portfolios.

Nowadays, it's all about Facebook Likes, LinkedIn endorsements and tweets.

What I notice to be severely lacking is the number of agencies who blog or create their own expert pieces outside their news feeds (which are clogged with client press release links… snore).

Coupled with that is the number of agencies and consultants who merely "syndicate" the content of others in their social media feeds.

So you read useful articles. We all do. But that can't be the sum total of your corporate communications. That's not what we'd recommend a client do (as you'll have seen in the Social Networking chapter earlier on).

The first issue, I understand. Content creation like blogging isn't easy. It's time-consuming and takes sustained resources and effort. And of course, if an agency isn't being asked to provide digital work then they may not need to show they are skilled in this arena. But I see plenty of consultancies publicising how knowledgable they are in SEO and how skilled they are in social media management, yet they don't even have their own online marketing strategy.

What the lack of content doesn't do is make me think any more of your company. It doesn't instil in me any faith that you can practice what you preach. That if I were a client parting with my hard-earned cash, that I would trust you to deliver in this rapidly-growing online world.

Or indeed, encourage me to work for you if I were a prospective job-seeker trying to choose between the many agencies this tiny land has spawned. So it has a knock-on effect as to the talent pool these companies will be providing to you, the client.

Bigger global agencies are better at content and creating a persona online. And I mean content in the widest sense of the word. It's not always an informative blog piece, sometimes it's merely a photo and caption of their charity bun sale in the office, an interview with staff, or a funny meme. But more often it's an in-depth look at current digital trends, how this impacts how they do business, followed up with case studies of clients they have worked with and the actual results they achieved for them.

A few agencies in Northern Ireland are good at it, proving that even small companies with tight resources can prove their worth by really engaging on social media. You then see this process replicated for their clients.

It's interesting to note, however, that the best examples of practicing-what-you-preach emerge from digital agencies or PR agencies who have the digital skill set in-house. I predicted last year that the traditional PR Agency would need to up its game if they want to remain key players or become industry leaders.

And this year, a plethora of PR houses have hired specialist digital staff, often tasked with their own branded content creation as much as producing work for clients.

Of course, procuring an agency isn't the only option open to you when it comes to buying support or outright outsourcing this aspect of your business. Indeed, it may not be the right option depending on what you need.

I've been in-house, in-agency and a freelance consultant, so it's fair to say I've seen the Pros and Cons of all three. And here I'll share what I've learned with you…

Staying In Control: In-House

This option sounds great but is hugely stressful and time-consuming. The work is varied and requires much more than allowing an intern to populate your social media channels.

A fully-functioning Communications department will involve research, strategy planning aligned to business objectives (and thus, evaluation at the end), building media relationships, writing (a lot!) producing every piece of content, news releases, social media posts; all planned and integrated into over-arching themes.

Plus day-to-day running of the projects including procuring designers, attending photo calls, dealing with website issues, answering media enquiries, online customer service, media monitoring… all of which is often done by just one individual.

This person will come to know your business inside and out. They will know instantly the brand personality and can be trusted.

Of course the first problem comes with finding, luring away and hiring such talent in an industry that is widely known to be under-skilled (on the Digital end of things at least).

Application forms won't cut it when recruiting this individual as most of us are skilled writers and spin doctors! They key is to set specific tasks and questions based on exactly what you want the person to do in the job.

Trust me, I've studied a Digital qualification - they don't (and can't) teach you to do the job practically.

It will be vital that this staff member is experienced. They will be the public face of your baby (i.e. your business).

Once you find this gem, the downside of having a role in-house is that you only get that one person's experience and skill set. You can't draw on a team of diverse and experienced people.

And inevitably, ambitious folk that we are, they will look to move on up the career ladder and, as a small company, you won't have many opportunities for them to do that. So expect turnover in the role every 2-3 years.

Freelancers & Consultants

This group bridges the in-house and the agency, while providing a middle ground price-wise too.

Consultants operate like full-service agencies, with retainer fees, regular clients and end-to-end delivery.

Freelancers, as a rule, tend to operate on a more short-term basis, consulting their time in terms of hours, days or short projects, and often subcontracting to the consultants and agencies as an additional resource.

They are obviously a cost-effective option, with the average copywriter or social media manager charging around £25-45 per hour. However they won't have the time and breadth to get to know your industry or company inside out on a one-off project and so there are certain tasks which may not be suited to them.

The freedom for you comes in the form of being able to contract out different aspects of the work that you can't do or don't want to do, without paying an agency or staff member to do everything, and only paying when you need the help.

You can do your own networking and simply contract out writing for example. Or you could call in help for events or launches at certain times of the year, confident that you can keep things ticking over the rest of the time.

With a consultant or freelancer as a business contact you can also benefit from their outsider opinion on your business as well as utilising their own list of contacts for other services you might need from people they have partnered with before, such as designers, event managers, or digital marketers.

However, a consultant is one person, juggling numerous tasks for numerous clients. If you need more support than the few hours a month you're paying them for, it may be time to call in the big guns...

Agencies

Agencies, being the traditional model since the Mad Men days of old, remain one of the first go-to options for new or small businesses requiring PR and Digital support.

Agencies provide access to high-end resources and tools. They can afford media monitoring programmes for example, that most small businesses can not.

They will be cut-throat environments for the most part, well versed in the media or digital arenas, depending on which type of agency you meet (I have yet to meet one that does both elements to an equally high standard, but individually they do different elements exceedingly well).

Trust me when I tell you that these organisations have a reputation for hiring the most ambitious, young and hungry folk and they get results alright.

So what's the downside?

Well you will need to think carefully about how you will manage the relationship with an agency. What is the biography and experience of the executives managing your account? How often do you expect them to work on your business and how often do you expect to be in contact?

Are you prepared to feed them regular information and content? Because without it, they will be seriously stunted in their ability to get results for you.

Cost is a big factor too, as agencies will be the most expensive option available to you when outsourcing.

It's important to weigh up what you will get from a retainer. If you pay a basic industry average of say £1,000 per month, it may well be worth it to you to not have to try to do everything in this book yourself.

But will you get everything you need in that? Possibly not, certainly not social media management which is very time consuming and is normally charged as an add-on.

And if your £1,000 equates, as it often does, to the basic 10-12 hours per month, with an account executive working on it who earns somewhere around £18,000 a year (just under £300 a week take-home) then their hourly rate is £7.50 and you're paying £100 an hour for it.

But simple maths is a crude way to look at it. We realise they have overheads, just like your business.

It's your call to weigh up how confident you are in all aspects of marketing your business in the new media and online world and valuing what each outsource option will bring to your bottom line.

How To Choose

The point is, the responsibility lies with you. You need to know what you need. Don't rely on a agency or consultant eager for new business to tell you what you need. Because undoubtedly they will tell you that you need only what they can give you.

I've worked with nearly all the agencies in my locality, bar a few. I have networked with and trained hundreds of in-house and freelance consultants. They are all different, in work style and industry experience.

They offer so much, individually, in their own unique way.

Just like this book is a reflection of my personal industry experience and what I've learned along the way. No two books would be the same.

So when you've reached the point of needing to outsource, where do you start to choose one?

Well here's what you don't do:

Don't automatically look for a team experienced in your sector, based on their existing clients. They may save time researching your industry media contacts but if your retainer is smaller than your competitors, you can guess who will get the cream of opportunities.

Likewise, don't write-off someone who doesn't usually work in your area. If this book has taught you anything it should be that the majority of expertise in this industry lies in the ability to mine new information, be it technical skill or contacts. As long as you like the work they've done before, they can augment it for your needs.

Don't be lured into paying a big retainer for the ease of a one-stop-shop unless it fulfils all your needs. As a freelancer, I have to be honest about my abilities, because the buck stops with me. I have no team to fall back on. I regularly advise people to seek out a Digital Marketer for skilled PPC or Facebook ads, hire a certain PR consultant for media coverage in an area unknown to me (such as The Arts), or hire a copywriter to create news articles and website content on technical subjects like Engineering. Their rates combined will probably still come in less than an agency retainer fee and you will be guaranteed more of their time and attention.

Likewise, don't tar all agencies with the one brush. There are some standout stellar ones emerging in Ireland who go above and beyond, who understand new concepts like startups and CrowdFunders and who don't follow traditional Senior Director structures, instead hiring a team of equals with a diverse skill set. They may well be what your business needs, even if they're outside your budget just now.

Don't let your ego make the decisions for you. By that, I mean the fact that I've turned away more prospective clients than I've taken on this year. Why? Because they initially approached me for PR but, after a more in-depth discussion about their business, what they really needed was improved SEO. Having their mugshot in the newspaper was going to make their Mum chuffed, but it wasn't going to bring them new customers who would ultimately Google their services before all else.

Don't be fooled by sales pitches. Some bigger teams will bring a host of big guns into a meeting with you and their experience will be impressive. But they may not be the people who will work on your account. If it is to be the Junior Executive, he/she may be very good (often the "work horses" are the more creative and digitally-skilled) but it is your job to double-check. Equally if they proudly show you a celebrity-filled campaign portfolio ensure you know what they can realistically deliver for you on your limited budget.

If you want to test an agency or consultant, you could send them an email or tweet out of office hours and see if they work on any kind of cover/rota scheme, as you'd expect in a 24-hour media world. And if they're disagreeing with you, challenging you or being brutally honest at the pitch stage, move your ego aside and recognise that they are a good service provider. Bad PR people will stroke your ego, but it won't get you results in the long run.

Don't think that I'm biased because I freelance. I spent many (award-winning) years in-house and was devastated to have to leave an agency role with one of the most exciting organisations

I'd seen in my local industry in years. There are pros and cons to each outsource option, depending on your unique needs.

My ultimate advice would be to find the people, not the logo, not the reputation, not the price, but the people who practice what they preach. The people you believe are as excited by your business as you are. The people you feel you could become friends with. The people who can show you examples of what they can help you to achieve.

And if they tell you they don't have time to do for their own business what they're claiming they can do for yours, then they either don't understand digital business tactics, or they don't need more work.

Because if they did, they would make the time.

Just like I advise you to do, now that you have all the knowledge:

Make the time.

Have a try yourself.

Go forth and (digitally) prosper!

And remember what I've taught you - the digital industry is ever-changing. Keep reading, learning and teaching yourself. Visit www.aCupOfLee.com for updated advice on all these top tips!

Printed in Great Britain
by Amazon